Against the Grain

"Against the Grain"

New Approaches to Professional Ethics

~

Edited by

Michael Goldberg

First Edition 1993

Trinity Press International
P.O. Box 851
Valley Forge, PA 19482-0851

Scripture quotations are from the New Revised Standard Version Bible, copyright 1989, Division of Christian Education of the National Council of the Churches of Christ in the United States of America and from *Tanakh: A New Translation of the Holy Scriptures According to the Traditional Hebrew Text,* copyright 1985, Jewish Publication Society of America, and are used by permission.

Cover design by Brian Preuss

Library of Congress Cataloging-in-Publication Data

Against the Grain : new approaches to professional ethics / edited by
    Michael Goldberg. — 1st ed.
        p.   cm.
    Includes bibliographical references.
    ISBN 1-56338-058-7
    1. Business ethics.   2. Professional ethics.   3. Religion and
ethics.   I. Goldberg, Michael, 1950–
HF5387.A38   1993
174'.4—dc20   93-3917
                                                                  CIP

Printed in the United States of America

93 94 95 96 97 98 6 5 4 3 2 1

To the memory of Charles Weltner

Contents

$\sim$

Introduction

After Watergate in the seventies and Wall Street in the eighties, the clamor for more ethical behavior in business and the professions in the nineties continues to grow ever louder in our society. That cry seems to be uttered with the frequency of a mantra whose mere repetition will somehow enable practitioners to ward off any breakdown in the ethics, practices, or historic aspirations of their professions. Should some practitioners nonetheless lose sight of their responsibilities, elder statesmen from their profession—joined by assorted moralists and social critics—stand ready to harangue these backsliders about their "professional duties" and the various rules and principles defining "professional conduct." Yet despite such exhortation—or because of it—thoughtful practitioners looking for moral guidance find that contemporary reflection on professional ethics typically offers precious little help.

This book's title represents a rejection of most of the current thinking on professional ethics—and a challenge to do things differently. The articles explore ways in which the notion of religious tradition may suggest new angles of vision from which to take a fresh look at professional ethics. Starkly put, a religious tradition, like a profession, involves a *community of practice*. For the professions, one aspect of that similarity is crucial: though religious communities and practices are in general rule-governed, they are at bottom *story-based*.

The Christian practice of the Eucharist, for instance, is performed according to certain rules specifying who may minister, when, and to whom. But the fact that Christians practice such a rite of reconciliation and forgiveness at all stems from the foundational Christian story of the life, death, and resurrection of Jesus Christ. Through the Eucharist, Christians do not merely reenact a key episode of that story, their Lord's

1

(last) supper. More basically, Christians enact their acceptance—their internalization and digestion—of Jesus' story-framed proclamation: "This is my blood of the new covenant, poured out for many for the forgiveness of sins" (Mt. 26:28). As Jesus' new covenant offers the prospect of a new community, so the Eucharist holds out to a community of practicing Christians nothing more nor less than the promise of transformation and renewal.

Indeed, such transformation and renewal is precisely what the notion of religion may offer communities of practicing lawyers, businesspersons, and other professionals. For the idea that we should see our work as more than occupation, our professional pursuit as more than career, and thus see both our work and profession as *vocation,* is itself a *religious* idea. If professionals can begin to see their lives as responses to some calling—that is, as responsibilities to those by whom they have been called, e.g., client, community, even Caller par excellence—then professionals' lives, together with their ethics, may start to embody stories more hopeful and more truthful than before.

For this reason, contributors to this volume have employed the categories of religion and narrative as methodological tools for grappling with professional ethics. To be sure, the tools they employ, though similar, are not identical; the contributors use narrative in the same way no more than they belong to the same religion. Nevertheless, their basic two-pronged approach to professional ethics by way of narrative and religion puts them and this book squarely at odds with most other work in the field, such that the work contained herein truly can be said to run "against the grain."

To see how the grain generally runs these days on matters of professional ethics, we need look no farther than two presentations given at a January 1992 conference at the University of Florida. The presentations reflect the intellectual emptiness and pragmatic fecklessness so prevalent at this time.

First, a paper by one of the world's most renowned moral philosophers, R. M. Hare, displayed what typically happens when academics address professional ethics issues: the issues—and their solutions—become *academic.* By using a fairly mundane and thus presumably unobjectionable example in his talk on business ethics, Hare sought to demonstrate the validity of the old moral chestnut that honesty is the best policy. Suppose, said Hare, that we were going out to buy a loaf of bread. We go to a bakery and pay one dollar for a one-pound loaf. The next day, however, we see another bakery charging only eighty cents for a one-pound loaf, and since that, of course, seems a better deal, we buy a loaf of bread there.

But, continued Hare, suppose we later learn that we had been cheated on the second loaf's weight, so that instead of having purchased a one-pound loaf for eighty cents, we had actually gotten a half-pound loaf! With that, Hare tried to drive home his point that honesty pays off. He maintained that if word were to get out about the dishonest baker's deceptive practice, his business would clearly suffer. Hare went on to contend that the town's honest bakers had both a moral and prudential interest in putting the cheater out of business, lest suspicion and consequent economic loss, however unjustified, fall on their bakeries as well. Hence, concluded Hare, honesty *is* the best policy. Q.E.D.

The problem with Hare's simple example is that it is too simple to be of much use to any businessperson confronting a far more complex world and moral life. Hare's example is so far removed from modern complexities that it must rely on a rather quaint picture of economic life in some idyllic hamlet. My point here is not the tired canard that professors live in ivory towers cut off from the real world. Rather, my claim is that for academics to function in the field of professional ethics *as professionals themselves*—as *learned* scholars—they must study and come to know various areas of professional endeavor with much more depth and understanding than they now typically display.

A more informed and hence *more truthful* illustration could have been drawn from a business such as the airline industry where, because of the large amount of capital investment required, there are relatively few competitors. In such an industry—which is in essence an oligopoly—whatever the keys to successful competition may be, competing on price is most definitely *not* one of them. Just witness the demise of all the airlines that have gone down in flames as they tried to fly their prices at lower and lower levels: People Express, Air Florida, America West, Continental. Although the government forbids outright collusion among airlines in setting prices, the various players can still easily learn about one another's fares (through media reports, advertising, travel agents) and set their own accordingly.

But if they do that, will they have engaged in any kind of dishonest or double-dealing business practice? While Americans might be able to achieve some consensus over what would be an excessive price for a one-pound loaf of bread, they could likely reach no such easy agreement about a "fair" price for a plane trip between, say, Atlanta and Cancun or Kankakee. Perhaps Hare would admonish us to push fares down as low as possible so that no one would be overcharged as in the selling of a half-pound loaf at one-pound prices. But as we noted above, more than a decade of deregulated, often cutthroat airfare pricing has created an airline graveyard. And as one airline after another has gone out of business, business at the unemployment office has increased as thousands of former airline employees queue up for welfare checks while millions of consumers line up to purchase ever-higher tickets from ever-fewer competitors. Hence, if I am an airline executive, what guidance does Hare have to offer? "Be honest" is not even remotely sufficient, for given the economic dynamics of my industry's pricing strategies, it is not at all clear *what counts as honesty,* let alone fairness.

I am not claiming that we contributors to this book have a clean, ready answer to such issues. Nevertheless, virtually all the writers represented here would likely respond that any answer will prove deficient unless it displays a keener grasp of the character and history of each professional community as well as of the larger communities those professions serve. Thus, Richard Vance's essay, "We Are All Pragmatists Now: The Limits of Modern Medical Ethics," argues that until we can give a coherent account of medicine *as a practice,* we will be in no position to put forward any cohesive theory of medical ethics. Vance should know. Besides being a medical ethicist at a teaching hospital, he is also a practicing pathologist. In fact, much of what this book has to say about professional ethics comes from people like Vance whose daily work joins *praxis* with *theoria,* knowing *how* with knowing *that.* Significantly, Vance's observations are not only far more insightful than those typically offered by moral philosophers like Hare, they are also a good deal less cheery. Indeed, if Hare's example illustrates the kind of moral counsel academic philosophers are prepared to give us—bromides like "Be honest," and commonplaces we should have learned at our mother's knee—our moral situation is far worse than Hare or his colleagues ever imagined.

The fact that our society's moral situation is indeed worse is reflected in the narrow scope of its moral discourse. Such discourse has become so focused on disparate rules and principles that we have been reduced to invoking moral platitudes. The legal ethicist Tom Morgan has remarked that when it comes to our moral counsel to professionals, we offer little more than the injunction, "Pull up your socks and try harder!" As Alasdair MacIntyre and others have pointed out, we wind up with such hollow moral abstractions as "universalizable rules," "principles of reason," "inherent rights," and "agent autonomy" because we live in a society with no coherent, shared "story."[1] We possess no single unifying narrative, whether biblical, historical, or otherwise, that can provide a common ground upon which to build our communal moral discourse and practice.

Instead, as heirs to many different story fragments—from the Bible, Aristotle's Greece, the Enlightenment—we possess only the fossil remains of once-thriving organic moral wholes. Because we tend to be unaware that these are only story shards, we fail to notice how frequently they do not fit together, but scrape against each other. They leave us not only with what MacIntyre calls our "interminable" moral debates over such issues as abortion and euthanasia, but also with the resulting frustration that leads us to view our opponents as maliciously stubborn or morally blind. At wit's end, we grasp at such moral talismen as "the sanctity of life" and "the quality of life." But lacking any larger background context or consensus to spell out concretely, non-arbitrarily what such generalities might mean, we are at a loss to specify how *in practice* professionals ought to apply them.

Once again, a paper delivered at our aforementioned professional ethics conference vividly illustrates the intellectual and pragmatic sterility arising from ethics proposals that ignore the centrality of stories for human endeavors like the professions, which depend on a *community of practice*. Two professors from Washington University in St. Louis made a presentation in which they claimed that using a Kohlbergian moral development scheme, they had produced a handy, surefire approach to teaching students how to make correct moral judgments in their work. With an air of scientific precision, the professors pointed to Kohlberg's highest stage of moral development, characterized by a universal commitment to freedom, fairness, and equality, as embodying the principles they wanted students to employ in their moral decision-making.

But how should their students morally assess the professional practice of Dr. Kevorkian, a.k.a. Dr. Death, who, appealing to those very principles of freedom, fairness, and equality, stands ready to help the sick commit suicide? Furthermore, how should those students morally judge physicians who oppose Kevorkian while appealing to the selfsame principles? Finally, in thinking about physician-assisted suicide, how should those students—and the rest of us—morally view Kohlberg and his ethical theory, given *his* suicide? Interestingly (and revealingly) the two professors had nothing to say about Kohlberg's death. Neither their (allegedly) freestanding analytical framework nor our story-impoverished society enables any of us to say much, if anything, coherent about the theoretical positions or actual lives of either Kohlberg or Kevorkian.

But our problem runs even deeper, for we do not have a coherent way to talk about ethics, nor to characterize the professions themselves. Not for nothing in our society do we come upon heated spats between people from different occupations arguing over whose is a "true profession" and whose is not. Of course, ours is a society that in one breath speaks of "the medical profession" and "the legal profession" and in the next of "professional wrestlers" and "professional hairdressers." On such an understanding, a professional is one trained in a certain art, which one then performs for a fee. But if that is all there is to being a professional, then, morally speaking at least, practitioners of "the world's oldest profession" are aptly named.

Classically, however—which is to say historically—the notion of a profession involved more than mere issues of training and compensation.[2] Professions were considered to *contribute to the common good the sorts of moral goods that no recognizably human community could live without.* Hence, medicine contributed the good of health, law the good of justice, and ministry the good of salvation. While specific conceptions of community and of the various moral goods needed to sustain community might differ from one society to the next, one thing remained constant: a concept of the common good standing at the core.

Indeed, prior to the Civil War, American society, too, had such a concept; its clearest, most memorable spokesman was Abraham Lincoln.[3] But following that war, Americans saw the emergence of an industrial society, as new social structures, such as the private corporation and the large law firm, appeared on the scene. The dominant social metaphor of earlier times, the town meeting, where civic-minded neighbors came together to form a consensus, was replaced by a new master image: the marketplace. Founded on no substantive common ends, the marketplace instead was built on common rules of procedure meant to keep the economic struggle "fair" among adversarial strangers. From the vantage point of the free market, American life could no longer be viewed as the expression of a social compact forged to pursue the common good, but rather as a series of private contracts licensing the pursuit of individual goods.[4] In such a society where talk of the common good has ceased to make any sense, how can we possibly continue to speak coherently about the professions, whose traditional *raison d'etre* was to contribute to such a good?

Nevertheless, for a Jack Sammons the professions still retain some vestigal memory of an earlier shared conception of the good. Indeed, because Sammons believes the professions might just be the only places in our society where such a shared conception remains, he reluctantly concludes that as a people we are inevitably thrown back on the professions for ethical guidance. Hence, his essay, "Rebellious Ethics and Albert Speer," contends that taking one's stand in the storied tradition of a profession may offer a moral atmosphere more sustaining to the moral life than that generally available in the larger society. Sammons believes the climate of the professions may well be healthier for the moral life than the thin air of individual moral protest. Such protest would have us imagine ourselves to be random "persons," detached from any larger story. But as Steven Crites noted long ago, our very sense of self stems from the story we perceive ourselves to be living out.[5] Consequently, if our stories and our identities are joined, we can no more live without a story than we can live without an identity. It is just a matter of *which* identity and *which* story we are going to be enacting in our lives.

William Willimon's article, "Clergy Ethics: Getting Our Story Straight," shows how a pastor and his counseling can be unwittingly co-opted by a story other than the Jesus-centered one which Christians have taken as formative for two millennia. Willimon reminds us that at the heart of a religious tradition stands a community with a narrative that can offer professionals provocative moral alternatives to those abroad in the culture.

My own essay, "Corporate Culture and the Corporate Cult," surveys the significance of religious community further, but from a very different standpoint. Discussing issues in business ethics, I claim that, for better or worse, many large companies come closer than anything else in contemporary American life to providing their employees with a sense of religious community, with all the attendant sacred stories, rites, and exemplars. In that respect, many of my essay's themes are "in conversation" with those of Sammons and Willimon. Hence, another novel, contrarian aspect of this book is its display of—and belief in—*interprofessional dialogue*. Indeed, if our analysis is correct in suggesting that America's fractured ethics reflect the shattered stories beneath them, then the "crises in ethics" among the various professions are only *different symptoms of the same disease*. If practitioners can talk across professional lines, they may gain a breadth of understanding that holds out a broader range of options for their engaging and resolving the ethical crises besetting them.

We hope that the spectrum of professions spanned by the book's contributors will serve as a token of the promise such interprofessional dialogue offers. Whereas most writing on professional ethics rounds up the usual suspects—a doctor, a lawyer, a journalist perhaps—this book reaches out to some heretofore un(der)represented professions. Thus, Senator John Danforth writes of professional politicians, claiming in his article, "The Point of Serving" that there can be no true service to the common good, no truly professional politics, without a commitment to truth-telling that takes precedence over the individual good of one's own reelection. For her part, Deborah Fernhoff writes from the perspective of another discipline usually absent from discussions of professional ethics: psychotherapy. In her essay, "The Valued Therapist," Fernhoff discusses the ways in which some psychologists have turned away from the old, allegedly "value-free" approach to working with clients; instead, they employ a more effective (and more efficient!) method requiring both therapist and patient to make explicit the religious perspectives and cultural 'myths" each brings to the psychotherapeutic setting. Nancey Murphy's contribution, "Creation, Cosmology, and Ethics," shows how an interactive relationship between science and theology may yield new, more subtle cosmologies with significant implications for scientists and others engaged in environmental ethics. Finally, Thee Smith suggests in his piece, "After Teaching: Wisdom," that a return to narrative as a primary mode of instructional discourse will enable those inside the academy as well as out to share in the kind of spiritually-powerful learning that transforms the self.

One more innovative feature of this book remains to be discussed. In the appendix is a worksheet meant to be an analytical tool for giving professional practitioners a start at understanding and, if necessary, changing the ethics and "values" of their organizations. The worksheet encompasses many of the concepts used throughout the essays in the book, such as story, virtue, and practice. Getting such data, though apparently simple, is nevertheless time-consuming; rightly telling and hearing complex stories is not done, as the Talmud puts it, "while standing on one foot." Working through the questions on the sheet will thus be like working through therapy, in which our lives become works-in-progress, where a central goal is ever-greater truthfulness. To paraphrase something once said by Stanley Hauerwas—cherished friend and teacher of several of the writers of this volume—we can only change the world we can see.[6]

I would like to add a special thanks to a friend I have known since boyhood, Christopher Brewster, for his invaluable assistance in lending a hand with the book at a crucial moment. In a similar vein, I want to state my gratitude to Steve Hilton. Finally, I must also thank Dr. Harold Rast of Trinity Press International for his support of this project. In a book on professionalism, an author cannot help but be grateful for the opportunity to work with an editor from the "old school" of publishing, someone true to his profession's highest ideals.

This book is dedicated to the memory of Charles Weltner, who was Chief Justice of the Georgia Supreme Court and who had originally agreed to be a contributor before illness made it impossible for that good man to keep his commitment. It was, I would wager, the only professional commitment Chief Justice Weltner ever failed to keep.

Charles Weltner's story has grown in familiarity since he received the 1991 "Profile in Courage Award" from the John F. Kennedy Library Foundation. In 1966, he was a thirty-nine-year-old, second-term Georgia congressman. One of only two Southerners to vote in favor of the 1964 Civil Rights Act, he had a promising political career and was running for reelection, having signed the Georgia Democrats' customary oath pledging support for all party nominees. However, when the party nominated segregationist Lester Maddox for governor, Weltner concluded that since he could neither violate his oath nor support Maddox, he would give up his office. He said, "I cannot compromise with hate. I cannot vote for Lester Maddox. . . . I will give up my office before I will give up my principles."

When Charles Weltner spoke of principle, he never had in mind principle *alone*. That is, he never based his judgment on some detached Kantian imperative or utilitarian maxim or bit of "black-letter" law. Rather, he saw principles against the backdrop of an unfolding story, a *history,* which he saw as his heritage and trust. That history was broader than just that of a Southerner—though it certainly embraced that story, as indicated by the political memoir he authored by that name. Nor was that history limited to the history of law—though it certainly included that, as shown by his frequent lament that law schools no longer required legal history. Nor in the end could that history even be contained within the sweep of biblical narrative—though it certainly encompassed that, as his mastery of ancient languages, interest in archaeology, and doctoral work in biblical pseudepigrapha made clear.

These different strands of history gave Charles Weltner a powerful story to carry on and carry out in his own life story. Living in our culture, he, like the rest of us, could not always hold those strands tightly intertwined; sometimes they unravelled, along with the coherency of his moral views. Hence, he was a man who was a staunch supporter of the death penalty despite its disproportionate application to poor blacks. However, he was also a man who filed lawsuits to overturn Georgia's election procedures meant to dilute the voting strength of the urban black poor. Perhaps the moral tie between Weltner's sense of history and *his* story was best delineated by his long-time friend, Senator Wyche Fowler, at his inauguration as Chief Justice:

> For Charles Weltner is not just a lawyer; he is a scholar of law and history. And his love of the ancient world tells a lot about him.
>
> How few of us understand our own age. We flip switches and push buttons without knowing the first physics formula, much less the forgotten theorems of antiquity. We try to wield the machinery of democracy—with too little notice of Jefferson, not to mention Montesqieu, Cincinnatus, or . . . Pericles.
>
> The roots of *this* man—all the way back to [the first Georgia Supreme Court] Chief Justice [Joseph Henry] Lumpkin [who was Weltner's great-great-grandfather]—run too deep for any . . . nonsense. History, the law, the code of honor and the code of conduct are all one in the mind of Charles Weltner.
>
> I believe he sees the broadest sweep, the true pilgrim's progress—not just the legal, but the spiritual, ethical, moral, and philosophical progress of humankind.

In the last part of his life, Charles Weltner was greatly concerned about raising the level of professionalism among lawyers. Lawyers and other professionals could do far worse than attend to the story told through Chief Justice Weltner's life. His is a story that reminds us that in the last analysis our ethics—professional and other—are not so much about our rules or decisions as they are about our lives themselves.

MICHAEL GOLDBERG

NOTES

1. Perhaps the most well-known expositions of the significance of narrative for ethics are to be found in Alasdair MacIntyre, *After Virtue* (Notre

Dame, IN: University of Notre Dame Press, 1981), and Stanley Hauerwas with Richard Bondi and David Burrell, *Truthfulness and Tragedy* (Notre Dame, IN: University of Notre Dame Press, 1977). Of particular interest also is Robert Coles, *The Call of Stories: Teaching and the Moral Imagination* (Boston: Houghton Mifflin Company, 1989). Coles tells of his use of various narratives in the moral and professional training of students pursuing diverse vocations.

2. For the best overview of the development of the professions, particularly in America, see Burton J. Bledstein, *The Culture of Professionalism* (New York: Norton, 1976).

3. Cf. Robert N. Bellah, Richard Madsen, William M. Sullivan, Ann Swidler, and Steven M. Tipton, *Habits of the Heart: Individualism and Commitment in American Life* (New York: Harper & Row, 1985).

4. Two fine accounts of the development of the legal profession during this period are in Lawrence M. Friedman, *A History of American Law,* 2nd ed. (New York: Simon & Schuster, 1987), and Robert Stevens, *Law School: Legal Education in America from the 1850s to the 1980s* (Chapel Hill, NC: University of North Carolina Press, 1983).

5. Steven Crites, "The Narrative Quality of Experience," *Journal of the American Academy of Religion* 39 (September 1971).

6. Cf. Stanley Hauerwas, *Vision and Virtue* (Notre Dame, IN: Fides Claretian, 1974), p. 102.

Corporate Culture and the Corporate Cult*

Michael Goldberg

I

As American business enters the last decade of this century, its corporate watchword might well be: *"The era of 'human capital' is upon us."*[1] The structural barriers of the past that protected companies—geography, regulation, technology, and scale—are all breaking down. The strategic question of the eighties was 'Where best to compete?'; the question for the nineties will be '*Who* can compete best?'[2] The previous agenda was dominated by financial matters such as economic forecasts and stock values; business strategies in the coming decade will be governed more and more by such matters of corporate culture as corporate vision and corporate values.

That nineties phenomenon may well imply another: at the end of the twentieth century some American corporations may constitute the closest thing our society has to community. Such companies form communities of their members by providing them with common goals, common procedures for attaining those goals, and common standards for marking success and failure. Unlike most other associations in contemporary American life, ranging from men's clubs to marriages, the corporate

*An earlier version of this article appeared in *A Virtuous Life in Business,* Oliver F. Williams and John F. Houck, eds. (Lanham, Md.: Rowman & Littlefield, 1992), 29–50.

community's existence depends on neither mutual admiration nor a spirit of volunteerism; businesspeople who find themselves in a corporate setting are not necessarily nor even primarily together because they like each other. Instead, such people are bonded by "a sense of reliance on one another toward a common cause. . . ."[3]

Such talk of joint reliance in pursuit of a common cause may call to mind medieval sagas of sacred quests for holy grails. No wonder. For some corporations hold out to their members a community of a particular kind: in fundamental ways, the community they present is a *religious* one.

Although speaking of a corporation as a religious community may at first sound shocking, we find among the earliest manifestations of corporations just that: namely, such corporate bodies as monasteries and bishoprics. St. Benedict, for example, wished to form a religious institution that was virtually self-contained, a kind of miniature society. Indeed, the very word "corporation" springs from the root *corpus,* signifying a "*body sharing a common purpose in a common name.*"[4]

Closer to our own time, several observers have noted the key role that corporate cultures play in shaping the attitudes and actions of those who inhabit them. But few—if any—have noticed a concept closely related to culture: *cult.* Both cult and culture trace their roots to a common etymological ancestor, *colere,* meaning "to cultivate or cherish." Indeed, for many late twentieth-century Americans, the corporate cultus is more cherished, more venerated, than any other institution, including their churches and synagogues. The corporation and its cult not only help construct the basic reality of their lives à la Geertz, but, à la Tillich, they also furnish those lives with the "ultimate concerns" of meaning, vision, and values. Consequently, for Americans such as these (i.e., people living in an increasingly atomistic, fragmented society), some corporations truly do create some overarching meaning. Moreover, "through their rituals, [such corporations] teach people how to behave, not just in their corridors of power but in the world at large."[5]

Whatever rituals, visions, or values have blossomed in the traditions of such corporations *cum* religious communities, the ground from which they have sprouted is the same as that for any other human community, whether religious or otherwise: a *story* of a corporate past arcing toward some future. For those who remain faithful to their storyline, the risk of faith is that the future will be one of blessing rather than of curse, of good fortune and not of doom.

II

In *After Virtue,* Alasdair MacIntyre calls attention to the centrality of stories for human life by reminding us that "I can only answer the question 'What am I to do?' if I can answer the prior question 'Of what story . . . do I find myself a part?'"[6] In other words, larger communal stories frame our individual life stories, thereby framing our identities as well. Often cast as histories, such communal narratives, by requiring that we look back at significant persons and events in the past, implicitly suggest characters and occurrences for us to look for in the future. In short, such stories impart to us a *vision.* That vision shows us a future in which, according to MacIntyre,

> certain possibilities beckon us forward and others repel us, some seem already foreclosed and others perhaps inevitable . . . . If the narrative of our [life] is to continue intelligibly . . . it is always both the case that there are constraints on how the story can continue *and* that within those constraints there are indefinitely many ways it can continue.[7]

Such classical communal stories therefore invite their hearers to think of themselves as participants in an embodied narrative quest toward some future goal or end.[8] As a consequence, these selfsame stories will also provide their hearers guidance in what will be "counted as harm and danger and . . . how success and failure, progress and its opposite, are understood and evaluated."[9] Thus, prominently depicted in these stories will be certain *recurring kinds of performances,* that is, *practices;* also strikingly displayed will be certain *habitual ways of performing those practices,* that is, *virtues.* For those who would embark on the quests recounted in the narrated traditions of story-based communities, practices and virtues are indispensable moral resources, because they have the power to "sustain us in the relevant kind of quest for the good by enabling us to

overcome the harms, dangers, temptations and distractions which we encounter, and which will furnish us with increasing self-knowledge and
increasing knowledge of the good [desired]."[10] Stories, by giving us a vision of communal quests toward some end accompanied by the requisite
practices and virtues, thereby give us our "values."[11]

Israel's exodus from Egypt is just such a story.[12] It is a narrative about
a quest embarked upon by a community-in-formation toward a common
goal—the fulfillment of a promise:

> The Lord said to Abram, "Go forth from your native land and from your
> father's house to the land that I will show you. I will make of you a great
> nation and I will bless you; I will make your name great, and you shall be
> a blessing. I will bless those who bless you and curse him who curses you.
> All the families of the earth shall bless themselves by you." (Gen. 12:1–3)

It is the dynamic of that promise's fulfillment which drives the narrative
forward. No matter how many twists and turns the storyline may take—
a Hebrew baby raised by the daughter of the Hebrews' genocidal enemy,
a speech-impeded man called to be spokesman par excellence, a forty-
year wilderness trek to kill off the generation just rescued!—certain outcomes are nevertheless precluded: Israel may turn back to Egypt no more
than she may worship a golden calf.[13] Instead, an altogether different
destiny is envisaged, an entirely different vision summoned up:

> Now then, if you will obey Me faithfully and keep My covenant, you shall be
> My treasured possession among all the peoples. Indeed, all the earth is Mine,
> but you shall be to Me a kingdom of priests and a holy nation. (Ex. 19:5–6)

But the narrated keeping of the promise does more than power the
story forward. It also calls into being a practice and a virtue absolutely
essential for the existence of the community of Israel; the practice is *remembering,* the virtue *faithfulness.* In the Exodus narrative, it is an act of
remembering that triggers the chain of events leading to Israel's eventual
deliverance:

The Israelites were groaning under the bondage and cried out; and their cry for help from the bondage rose up to God. God heard their moaning, and God remembered his covenant with Abraham and Isaac and Jacob. (Ex. 2:23–24)

Later, another act of remembering preserves Israel when, though recently delivered from Egyptian servitude and pledged to serve the Lord, she renders him false service instead:

The Lord spoke to Moses, "Your people . . . have acted basely. They have been quick to turn aside from the way that I enjoined upon them. They have made themselves a molten calf and bowed low to it . . . . Now, let me be, that my anger may blaze forth against them, and that I may destroy them. . . ."

But Moses implored the Lord his God, saying, "Let not your anger, O Lord, blaze forth against your people. . . . Turn from your blazing anger, and renounce the plan to punish your people. Remember your servants, Abraham, Isaac, and Jacob, how you swore to them . . . , 'I will make your offspring as numerous as the stars of heaven, and I will give to your offspring this whole land of which I spoke, to possess forever.'" And the Lord renounced the punishment he had planned to bring upon his people. (Ex. 32:7–8, 10–14)

For the community of Israel, remembering past promises is indispensable for realizing whatever promise the future may hold.

But remembering the past, like keeping a promise, requires one virtue above all others: faithfulness. In the Hebrew Bible, the word that typically expresses that virtue is *chesed*. The term, appearing in one form or another over two hundred times in scripture, has at bottom a specific, quasi-technical meaning: "covenantal loyalty."[14] In the Exodus narrative, the paradigmatic exemplar of that virtue is God. Thus, in an act of covenant renewal following Israel's transgression with the calf, God reveals to Moses his hallmark character trait, his chief virtue, which enables him to renew the covenant in the first place: "The Lord! A God compassionate and gracious, slow to anger, rich in covenantal loyalty [*chesed*], showing faithfulness [*chesed*] to thousands . . ." (Ex. 34:6–7). As important,

Moses has whatever authority and leadership he possesses precisely because in many ways similar to God he, too, displays that singular virtue.
As depicted in the Exodus narrative, neither God nor Moses is particularly charismatic, or particularly eloquent, or particularly good at "managing" people.[15] And yet, they both excel at steadfastly persevering to
realize the ends they seek. Since Israel's continued existence depends on
just such steadfast devotion, God and Moses are, not surprisingly, the
heroes of the story that Israel tells from generation to generation.

Are there similar stories to be told—and heard—in corporate
America?

III

> For those who hold them, shared values define the fundamental character of
> their organization . . . that distinguishes [it] from all others . . . . [Such
> values] create a special sense of identity . . ., giving meaning to work as
> something more than . . . earning a living. . . . Sometimes managers
> refer explicitly to . . . these values in [guiding] subordinates. . . . *New
> people may be told stories about the company's past that underline the importance of
> these values to the company.*[16]

As in any corporate cult, General Electric's employees are deeply
devoted to its values, and in any recitation of those values, the company's
motto stands as the central tenet of its corporate creed: "Progress Is Our
Most Important Product." Yet even more fundamental than that corporate article of faith are General Electric's stories about the GE heroes, the
GE *saints,* who gave rise to that creed *by embodying it.*

One of their corporate saints is Thomas Edison, a figure revered not
only in GE's pantheon of heroes, but in the larger American society as
well. Virtually every American schoolchild knows the story of Edison
conducting experiment after experiment to find the right filament for
the electric light. And virtually every GE employee knows the story of
Edison developing the vehicle for simultaneous two-way telegraphic
communication: after spending twenty-two consecutive nights testing
twenty-three different duplexes, he finally invented one that worked.[17]

Another GE saint is Charles Steinmetz, a man whose life coincided with Edison's in many ways. He worked in Edison's lab, which he ran after Edison left.[18] Like Edison, Steinmetz suffered from a physical disability.[19] Like Edison, Steinmetz also played a large part in GE's growth as a company for he "brought alternating current into electrical systems of the world."[20] And as with Edison, stories about this work at GE germinated values which, along with their corporate exemplar, are revered to this day, as the following episode reported by one of the authors of *Corporate Cultures* makes clear:

> We drove by the General Electric Research Lab where—in an earlier era and building—Charles Steinmetz had conducted his experiments. The driver of the car motioned to the building and said, "Sometimes I get the feeling I can still see the lights on in there and Steinmetz working away." For the driver, and for other employees of GE *who never knew Steinmetz,* he still was a strong influence. . . .[21]

Not for nothing is *inventing* GE's cardinal practice[22] while *persistence*[23] is its cardinal virtue.

But Steinmetz also plays a saintly role in GE's lore in another way. He is responsible for creating the vision that stands at the heart of the company's story-based self-understanding as a community of inventive engineers and scientists with *close personal ties* to one another:

> Whenever young engineers joined GE, Steinmetz would invite them home for the weekend in order to learn, sincerely and without political intent, what kind of people they were. Once he adopted one of GE's leading engineers as his own son—and the man's whole family. They all moved into Steinmetz's house and lived with him for twenty years.[24]

With this bit of hagiography as background, General Electric nurtures a corporate cult which emulates the saintliness of Steinmetz through fostering supportiveness, loyalty, and respect among peer-group members.

Thus, like vibrant religious communities, some corporations have stories in which a venerated past bears promise for the future. In fact, many writers have suggested that companies displaying high financial performance and potential are precisely those with powerful narrative traditions.[25]

But is this account of the implications of story-based values for corporations, like some medieval morality play, a story too good to be true?

IV

MacIntyre would almost certainly answer yes. For him, while classical societies tended to reflect a single unified—and unifying—core narrative, modern culture reflects many different story fragments, thereby shattering our moral vision. Corporate life, for its part, fragments the moral life even more:

> Within any one large formal organization not only variety, but incoherence is to be found [since] corporate structures fragment consciousness and more especially moral consciousness.[26]

> Corporate existence . . . presupposes a separation of spheres of existence, a moral distancing of each social role from each of the others.[27]

In MacIntyre's view, corporate life splits the moral life into (at least) two distinct and incompatible realms: the individual corporate employee governed by utilitarian considerations, and the family member or citizen whose moral considerations are anything but utilitarian.[28] Consequently, for MacIntyre, the corporation, far from providing the closest thing our society has to community, is rather the institutional embodiment of a modern, individualistic ethos—the very antithesis of any genuine notion of community.

And yet, MacIntyre may well have gotten his labels reversed. For it could also be that in contemporary American society, the corporation in its basic structure and daily operation is the last bastion of any truly functioning community, while modern politics and the modern family run on little more than fleeting individual preferences and fickle personal desires.[29] As MacIntyre himself admits, corporate organization [must] be conceived in terms of roles and not of persons. Any role, any position, will be filled from time to time by different persons. . . . Correspondence for example is conducted with this or that office of the organization and not—except accidentally—with individuals. Hence the formal character of bureaucratic correspondence; hence the importance of files. Each file has a history [i.e., *a narrative*] which outlives that of the individuals who contribute to it.[30]

Indeed, many observers have taken note of the role that so-called excellent companies play in creating an entire reality for those working in them; even more than that, for many corporate employees, the reality thus created catches them up in something transcendent, even bordering on the religious. As Tom Peters has remarked in his best-selling book, *In Search of Excellence,*

By offering *meaning* as well as money, [the excellent companies] give their employees a *mission* as well as a sense of feeling great. Every man becomes a pioneer, an experimenter, a leader. The institution provides *guiding belief* and creates a sense of excitement, *a sense of being part of the best* . . . .[31]

In fact, at a time when the general culture provides little or no stability regarding values, corporations may play an especially crucial role by providing "structure and standards and a value system in which to operate."[32] In just that way, "corporations may be among the last institutions in America that can effectively take on the role of shaping values."[33]

Nevertheless, MacIntyre might still object that within the corporation values are not shaped but shattered as mixed signals are sent regarding them, so that the workplace is pervaded by the same moral chaos as any other place in contemporary American society:

Unfortunately the very same quality is often presented in one guise as a virtue, in another as a vice. The same executive is characteristically required to be meticulous in adhering to routines . . . *and* to show initiative. . . . Expecially [sic] perhaps among upwardly mobile middle management, contemporaries in the organization are presented at one and the same time as those *with* whom he or she is expected to cooperate and *against* whom he or she is expected to compete.[34]

Such conflicting imperatives, however, need not *necessarily* indicate moral anarchy. On the contrary, their conflict may arise in the first place precisely because they both spring from a moral outlook more fundamentally shared than shattered. In *Antigone,* for instance, the protagonist is faced with the dilemma of two apparently incommensurate moral claims: those calling her to honor her familial and religious obligations to bury her dead brother versus those calling her to keep her political obligations to deny burial to a traitor to the state. As a consequence, no matter how Antigone acts, her act can and will appear at one and the same time both a display of virtue—loyalty—and of vice—betrayal. Yet we must not miss the fact that this conflict between moral obligations in *Antigone* grows out of a unified, coherent moral vision in which life, its values, and its goods are understood principally in terms of concrete relationships, roles, and duties rather than abstract principles, rights, and "oughts."[35]

Similarly, the underlying tension between cooperation and competition in corporate life may stem from a deeper shared commitment to a common goal or good. We can think, for example, of a high school basketball team in which competition between team members exists side-by-side with cooperation for the sake of realizing a common purpose. In the context of practice, for instance, team skills such as the fast break and the zone defense, which demand cooperation among team members, co-exist with competition between individuals to increase their respective amounts of playing time or to crack the starting lineup. What must not be overlooked is that *both* cooperation *and* competition must be employed if the team itself is to achieve excellence, especially the excellence needed to be a champion prevailing over all opponents. So, too, if a company wants to achieve preeminence over other companies, its members must learn cooperation as well as competition.

But MacIntyre, undaunted, might still object that where achievement of excellence is equated with achievement of victory, any notion of virtue is summarily defeated, along with any claims to moral seriousness made on behalf of the corporation. For excellence and victory, though closely related, are nevertheless distinct concepts: after all, it is possible *to be excellent yet lose*. To see the difference between being excellent and being victorious, just look, says MacIntrye, at "the Spartan sacrifice at Thermopylae."[36]

But witness, too, the fact that even the excellent high school basketball team can lose through poor officiating costing it a crucial free-throw opportunity or through poor grades costing it the services of its star. Likewise, an excellent corporation may incur or even choose to court loss(es) in order to maintain certain standards of excellence: just witness the case of Johnson & Johnson during the Tylenol scare.

In the fall of 1982, seven people died when they swallowed Extra-Strength Tylenol capsules laced with cyanide. At the time, Tylenol was the top-selling health and beauty aid product in the United States.[37] Its corporate parent, Johnson & Johnson, had built the company's reputation on trust and responsibility, going back to its founding as an innovator in supplying sterile surgical dressings. Now, J&J was faced with the very real possibility that if it acted in a trustworthy and responsible fashion, it might well lose not only its premier product in the marketplace, but a significant slice of its total corporate revenues as well.

Nevertheless, within the first few days following the poisonings, the company, under the leadership of its chairman, James Burke, withdrew virtually its whole Tylenol line from market shelves and ceased all Tylenol advertising. Within a week, J&J stock had dropped about twenty percent, amounting to a paper loss of $2 billion. But said Burke, "It's important that we demonstrate that we've taken every single step possible to protect the public. . . ."[38] Hardly, it would seem, the words of someone blind to the difference between excellence and winning.

As events wore one, Burke stayed the course he had set. The consensus of his advertising consultants was that the Tylenol name was dead, and many, including media maven Jerry Della Femina, were adamant that the Tylenol name had to be changed before the product could be reintroduced. But Burke and J&J held firm. Wayne Nelson, J&J Company Group chairman, remarked, "It would almost be an admission of guilt . . . to walk away from that name."[39] Echoing Nelson, Burke said on the *Donahue* show,

> It seems to me that there is a certain not-playing-it-straight with the con-
> sumers on that one. If you are going to sell Tylenol, to sell it under a name
> other than its own name is kind of asking you to change your name after
> you've had a serious disease. . . .[40]

Throughout the whole affair, Burke and J&J stuck to their conviction that informing and protecting the nation would eventually result in "an eminently fair decision about the future of Tylenol."[41] In the end, the company saw its commitment to excellence in providing reliable health care vindicated. Within a year of the crisis, Tylenol had regained over ninety percent of the market it had enjoyed prior to the tragedies.[42] And in a *Fortune* magazine poll for America's most admired companies, J&J won top honors for its commitment to community and environmental responsibility.[43]

Even so, however, MacIntyre might once more mount a protest: the corporate practices of even a company like J&J have no real moral power or depth to them, because none of the goods pursued through those practices is *internal* to them. That is, in the course of pursuing the standards of excellence appropriate to and definitive of J&J's business activities, no good intrinsically related to such activities is realized; nor, for that matter, is any human power to achieve excellence or any human conception of the good involved systematically extended.[44] At best, only certain external or contingent goods are realized, such as money or power.

But the matter is not so easily settled. If we recall for a moment the key practice at General Electric—inventing—we discover that the chief good internal to the practice is the very one named in the company's motto: progress. And as GE's corporate story makes clear, progress is a good which would be difficult if not impossible to achieve without invention and the virtue necessary to sustain that practice, namely, persistence. As for J&J, it is a company at whose heart stands a *Credo*, a corporate catechism of convictions concerning its responsibilities to its customers, its employees, its community, and its shareholders—in just that order. To provide products and services in pursuit of health—an internal good if ever there was one—J&J must cultivate exactly those virtues it demonstrated during the Tylenol crisis: trustworthiness, practical wisdom, and courage.[45]

MacIntyre has pointed out that "in the ancient and medieval worlds the creation and sustaining of human communities—of households, cities, and nations—is generally taken to be a practice. . . ."[46] And so, too, ought we to take the creation and sustaining of certain corporate communities in the modern world. Hence, all moral misgivings regarding the corporation in its modern form would seem to be unwarranted.

Or are they? Before answering, we would be wise to hear the whole story of the rise of the modern American corporation.

V

"Are the vultures still out there?"—[Former] Drexel staffer, sneering at reporters as she walked out the door [following the firm's announcement of bankruptcy] "Vultures? Look who's talking."—Security guard (*Time,* 26 February 1990, p. 46)

Earlier we spoke of monastic communities as among the first corporations, as bodies of persons joined to pursue a common enterprise.[47] Such bodies, however, were interested in benefitting not only their own members but others as well. As Trachtenberg and Foner have reminded us, "It was assumed, as it is still in nonprofit corporations, that the incorporated body earned its charter by serving the public good."[48] Similarly, the authors of *Habits of the Heart* have pointed out that "incorporation [was] a concession of public authority to a private group *in return* for service to the public good. . . ."[49] Again, from the time of the earliest monastic orders, these corporate communities sought to contribute to the common good beyond the monastery walls. For example, because of "the paramount obligations of charity toward one's fellow man," St. Basil sought to establish his fourth-century monasteries "in towns instead of in desert wastes," while his forerunner, Pachomius, gathered his *Koinonia* or monastic community a century earlier out of a broader commitment to "the service of humankind."[50]

Clearly, such corporate models presupposed a model of society in which it made sense to speak of "the common good." But as American society became more and more industrialized following the Civil War, notions of the common good became less and less coherent. The bonds among Americans, both political and economic, grew increasingly attenuated. In the earlier life of the Republic, the dominant social metaphor was the town meeting, where all joined in an effort to reach consensus to pursue a common good. After the Civil War, the regnant image became the marketplace, where each pursued his or her own good. Indifferent or even hostile to the goods pursued by others, individuals were bound to others only by a few thin procedures meant to ensure that competition was—at least minimally—"fair."

Such was the social climate that spawned the modern business corporation. As Lawrence Friedman has noted in the late nineteenth century, "the overriding need was for an efficient, trouble-free device to aggregate capital and manage it in business, with limited liability and transferable shares."[51] Here the idea of "limited liability" is crucial, for the novel legal fiction giving the corporation the status of a "person" meshed perfectly with the social fabric of the times. In an age celebrating laissez-faire competition among rugged individuals, concocting a "super-individual" to join the fray was a master stroke. Better still, if the fray proved too hot and the adversaries too strong, then even though the corporation's legal person might be bested, its human persons, still shielded by the doctrine of limited liability, could withdraw unscathed with their own resources intact. As a result, incorporation, which once had been a rare privilege granted only by special charter for the sake of the common good, became an ever-present right, routinely available by application to any private enterprise—which could remain oblivious to any good but its own.[52]

VI

Accordingly, in a society where the notion of a common good has long since died, to find corporations acting without any regard for such a good is hardly surprising. Why, for instance, should anyone be surprised to find R. J. Reynolds attempting to regain lost cigarette sales by targeting blacks and young women in its advertising for new brands? In the fragmented, atomistic America of the late twentieth century, the burden of making a *coherent* moral argument is heavier for RJR's critics than it is for the company.

In its earlier days, of course, the company at least displayed commitment to those who fell within the orbit of its own corporate community. It provided adequate day care for workers' children, it offered RJR stock and liberal loans to its employees, and it gave generously to its hometown of Winston-Salem. And yet, as it continued to flourish in a culture which had increasingly lost sight of any *shared* good, RJR's commitments to share even with those in its own purview weakened. Thus, in connection with the RJR Nabisco takeover, over five thousand employees were eventually thrown out of work as the company virtually pulled out of Winston-Salem. In the leveraged buyout's aftermath, former RJR employees in Winston-Salem were besieged by brokers offering to buy their now highly valuable stock. In response, the townspeople asked incredulously, "You want to buy *stock?*" Explained Nabley Armfield, a local stockbroker, "You have to understand. Reynolds wasn't a stock. It was a *religion.*"[53]

But to the extent that American culture makes corporations like RJR Nabisco unsurprising, to just that extent, the corporate culture of a company like Johnson & Johnson is truly astonishing for binding the company to some larger, shared notion of the good. Like some religious order formed in another time and place, the Johnson & Johnson community lives by a *Credo:*

> We are responsible to the communities in which we live and work and to the world community as well. We must be good citizens—support good works and charities and bear our fair share of taxes. We must encourage civic improvements and better health and education. We must maintain in good order the property we are privileged to use, protecting the environment and natural resources. .

For J&J, these words are not some part of a dead doxology intoned as an ancient, fossilized rite. Instead, it is a living text which is revised periodically to keep J&J's corporate vision alive and vital. Hence, looking back on the "Tylenol nightmare" in which "literally dozens of people [had] to make hundreds of decisions in painfully short periods of time," James Burke could say with wholehearted conviction, "All of us . . . truly believe that the guidance of the Credo played *the* most important role in our decision-making."[54]

Nor are J&J and Burke alone in witnessing to a corporate life with striking similarities to certain aspects of religious life; they are joined by Herman Miller, Inc., and its chairman, Max De Pree. In the previously-mentioned *Fortune* listing of the nation's most admired companies, Herman Miller ranked ninth overall while taking sixth place for management excellence. In a newspaper interview, De Pree expressed his belief that one reason for America's lack of leadership "is that people have felt it was OK to put themselves ahead of the common good." He further noted that leadership is not a question "of techniques . . . but of what is in the heart," and that "corporations can and should have a redemptive purpose. . . ." De Pree's convictions about the corporation are nothing if not religious—especially this one: "Being faithful to a set of beliefs is more important than being successful."[55]

That claim, perhaps more than any other, raises the question whether some forms of corporate life can genuinely be considered as instances of the religious life. Would any corporation be willing to remain faithful to its values *even unto death?* If doing good and doing well do not necessarily go hand-in-hand, then corporations may need to weigh carefully the stories they live out: not all of them may have happy endings.

VII

Stories and values are not only sources of corporate performance; they are also constraints against it:

> Although [shared values] provide a source of clear common understanding in a business, they also constitute a constraint. When a company with strongly held values finds that [it has] lost marketplace or economic relevance, it generally has great difficulty adjusting successfully.[56]

A storied past thus not only *informs* us but, displaying a vision to guide our present and future, also *forms* us in the way we envisage our world and our options for acting in it. There is a reason why some seventy percent of corporate mergers fail, as companies find themselves unable to merge their separate and often incompatible storylines into a new ongoing narrative.[57] In such circumstances, corporate stories may spell death instead of life.

In the last analysis, the most basic test of any story, whether corporate or religious, is the kind of life that it produces—indeed, if it produces any life at all. Stories die when their communal embodiments do—which is only fitting justice. Hence, without Zeus worshippers, what are the stories of Zeus *but* stories? Granted, it may take a relatively long time for a community and its culture to see whether the story they have been living out may actually be leading to their dying out. Corporate cultures, however, may come by such knowledge more quickly with the rapid feedback provided by the marketplace. That feedback may carry with it possible correctives to prevent the company's story from having reached its final chapter. Thus, at the height of the Tylenol crisis, Burke told a press conference:

> We consider it a moral imperative, as well as good business, to restore Tylenol to its preeminent position in the marketplace. It is ironic that the job of rebuilding Tylenol is made more difficult because we all . . . did our job of informing and protecting the nation so efficiently. In the final analysis, we believe that the American consumer . . . will make an eminently fair decision about the future of Tylenol.[58]

Burke had faith that J&J's willingness to continue to live out its traditional storyline would be matched by the marketplace's willingness to let the company live on. J&J's willingness to act on that article of faith was what made its Credo credible.

Consequently, to dismiss business ethics such as J&J's as "*merely* utilitarian" is unwarranted. When executives like Burke "bet the company," they take nothing less than a risk of faith. In that regard, faith such as theirs may well resemble that of some religious communities during times of persecution, as reflected, for example, by this teaching from Jewish tradition:

> At a time of persecution when . . . decrees are issued against Israel aimed at abolishing their religious practice . . . , then let [a Jew] suffer death and not breach even one of . . . the commandments.[59]

Jewish tradition here makes sense precisely to the extent that there *is* a truly steadfast King of Kings to come to Israel's rescue before the life of the last Jewish man or woman is given up. If Jews act on this teaching, and the whole Jewish people subsequently perishes, then though the teaching may have been foolish, it will most assuredly *not* have been utilitarian. And the same could have been said about the Credo's teaching had J&J perished during the Tylenol crisis.

And yet, for all the virtues and all the faith that a company like Johnson & Johnson has shown, the virtues and the faith displayed though in certain key ways religious, are in no way *biblical*.[60] For neither their "structurings of reality" nor their ultimate concerns are finally unified with the One, who according to the Bible's story, has made all of life *one corpus,* sustained it, and for Christians at least redeemed it. In contrast, for many contemporary corporate communities, the horizons of their moral vision typically extend no farther than the boundaries of their market. Although J&J issued Tylenol recalls and warnings in its U.S. market, it took no such steps in its foreign markets, either because it knew conclusively that no contaminated Tylenol had been sold there—or, as may be more likely, its potential legal liability was not as high there. By comparison, a community whose vision has been expanded by the lenses provided by biblical narrative may be able to see *the world as a corporate whole* with the blessing of life offered as a common good above any individual partial goods.

Yet modern corporations tussling in the marketplace have no goods to offer but partial—and often conflicting—ones. In the pursuit of such limited goods, companies may ask unlimited commitment from their employees; indeed, it may be precisely the most conscientious companies which ask for the most commitment, whether an Edison-like dedication to round-the-clock inventing or a Credo-like fidelity to putting one's customers above all else. And yet, such commitment, even in the best of contemporary corporate communities and even with all the attendant piety, still falls short of being singleminded, wholehearted devotion to God.

One last reference to Johnson & Johnson may prove illuminative. During one of the company's periodic reviews of its Credo, Burke wanted to include an explicit reference and commitment to God. Others in the company, however, talked him out of it, warning against the possibility of a consumer backlash, and the idea was dropped. Burke and J&J, it would seem, made their choice of Mammon over God. Hence, whatever practices commitments such as J&J's may engender, those whose corporate vision has been shaped by biblical narrative—Jews, Christians, Muslims—may recognize such practices by another name: idolatry.

At present, such a biblical vision may be particularly difficult to attain, not merely because the biblical notion of idolatry seems so hopelessly anachronistic, but more fundamentally because the very corporations engaged in idol worship appear in many other ways to be so virtuous, so admirable, so noble. But, after all, that is the way it is with *noble pagans.* For them, religious practice does not consist of child sacrifice, nor do their values find expression in drunken orgies. Instead, virtue for such noble ones as these lies in a kind of honorable polytheism; that is, in paying due homage to the many gods, the many powers, and the many roles at work in the agora and the forum.

Thus, as America's corporate communities move into the first century of the next millenium, they may well carry with them religious values reminiscent of the first century of the first millenium. Those values, of course, stem from a story that in fundamental ways differs from one called "biblical." Consequently, no matter the millenium, no matter the community, the bottom-line issue remains the same: In which story and in which values ought we to invest our lives?

NOTES

1. Robert A. Irvin and Edward G. Michaels III, "Core Skills: Doing the Right Things Right," *The McKinsey Quarterly* 25 (Summer 1989), 10.

2. Ibid., 8.

3. Warren Bennis and Burt Nanus, *Leaders* (New York: Harper & Row, 1985), 83.

4. Alan Trachtenberg and Eric Foner, *The Incorporation of America: Culture and Society in the Gilded Age* (New York: Hill and Wang, 1982), 5; emphasis added.

   As for St. Benedict, his Rule gives "directions for the formation, government, and administration of a monastery and for the spiritual and daily life of its monks. . . . The Rule provides for an autonomous, self-contained community (66). . . . The monastery of the Rule is a microcosm containing inmates of every age and condition. . . ." (*The New Catholic Encyclopedia,* s.v. "Benedictine Rule," by B. Colgrave.)

5. Terrence E. Deal and Allen A. Kennedy, *Corporate Cultures* (Reading, MA: Addison-Wesley Publishing Co., Inc., 1982), 83. Though subtitled *The Rites and Rituals of Corporate Life,* the book contains precious little that approaches corporate life from the vantage point of religious life, or for that matter, religious studies. Instead, the volume and its bibliography are top-heavy with standard fare of business organization.

   Let me be clear here. My point is *not* that corporate life can be understood *only* from the perspective of religion; obviously, it can be analyzed from other standpoints as well—economics, sociology, social psychology, and the like. However, I am suggesting that various forms of religious life may offer rather fruitful ways for thinking about certain instances of corporate life, together with their visions and their values. In that respect, my primary task in this essay is more descriptive than prescriptive.

6. Alasdair MacIntyre, *After Virtue* (Notre Dame, IN: University of Notre Dame Press, 1981), 201.

7. Ibid., 200–201.

8. Ibid., 203.

9. Ibid., 135.

10. Ibid., 204.

11. I have set the word values in quotes to call attention to the fact that for ethics, that notion reflects a particularly modern understanding—namely, that in the last analysis, there are no moral goods or standards apart from individual preferences, desires, and wants. For powerful critiques of this position, cf. MacIntyre, Chapter 2, "The Nature of Moral Disagreement

Today and the Claims of Emotivism," and Allan Bloom, *The Closing of the American Mind* (New York: Simon & Schuster, 1987), 60–61.

The fact that American business as a whole tends to use "values" as synonymous for—and to the virtual exclusion of—other terms such as "ethics," "goods," and "standards" indicates that even for the corporation, an institution whose pre-modern motifs can still be heard, the trope of modernity is nevertheless inescapable.

12. See my *Jews and Christians, Getting Our Stories Straight* (Philadelphia: Trinity Press International, 1991).

13. Cf., e.g., Ex. 16:3, 17:3, and 32:25–35.

14. See Nelson Glueck, *[Ch]esed in the Bible,* trans. A. Gottschalk (Cincinnati: Hebrew Union College Press, 1967). Even if one prefers a less technical rendering of *chesed,* such as the RSV's "steadfast love," the term's basic thrust remains the same: faithful devotion.

15. See MacIntyre's description on 29 of the manager and therapist as embodying quintessentially modern roles which enable them to manipulate people to achieve certain ends, without regard for any moral concerns about such manipulation or such ends.

16. Julien R. Phillips and Allen A. Kennedy, "Shaping and Managing Shared Values," *McKinsey Staff Paper* (December 1980), 4; emphasis added.

17. Ibid., 11.

18. Deal and Kennedy, 45.

19. Steinmetz was crippled while Edison, having had his ears "boxed" as a child, suffered from a serious hearing loss.

20. Deal and Kennedy, 8.

21. Ibid., 47.

22. For a discussion of the relationship between practices and goods, see MacIntyre, 175, and my discussion on 24.

23. In fact, much of the current literature on leadership points to persistence as the outstanding character trait—that is, virtue—of those considered leaders. See Deal and Kennedy, 46; Bennis and Nanus, 45, 47, 187–188; Phillips and Kennedy, 18, 19; and Nigel Williams, "Managing Values on Wall Street," keynote speech to the Securities Industry Association Conference, 29 October 1987, 9.

Perhaps a necessary though not sufficient condition for any leader is a single-minded willingness to act out a vision and live out a story. Tom Peters, referring to the work of Bennis and Nanus, points out that leaders have clear visions, which are "lived with almost frightening consistency. . . ." (*Thriving On Chaos: Handbook for a Management Revolution* [New York: Perennial Library, 1987], 631.) That observation may help to remind us that corporate communities, particularly in their early days, are often like religious cults—that is, they are tightly organized around a central person, *the cult figure*. If that person is a cult figure like Jesus of Nazareth, well and good; if, however, that person is a cult figure like Jim Jones. . . .

24. Deal and Kennedy, 45.

25. Ibid., 7, 30. Cf. also Williams, 5; Phillips and Kennedy, 2, 12; and Alan Wilkins, "Organizational Stories as an Expression of Management Philosophy" (Ph.D. dissertation, Stanford University, 1978).

26. Alasdair MacIntyre, "Corporate Modernity and Moral Judgment: Are They Mutually Exclusive?" in *Ethics and Problems of the 21st Century,* eds. K. E. Goodpaster and K. M. Sayre (Notre Dame, IN: University of Notre Dame Press, 1979), 122.

27. Ibid., 126.

28. Ibid., 126–27.

29. Regarding contemporary politics, MacIntyre himself has written, "Modern politics is civil war carried on by other means." (*After Virtue,* 236) As for modern family, see Robert N. Bellah, Richard Madsen, William Sullivan, Ann Swidler, and Steven M. Tipton, *Habits of the Heart: Individualism and Commitment in American Life* (New York: Harper & Row, 1985), Chapter 4, "Love and Marriage." See also Christopher Lasch's *Haven in a Heartless World: The Family Besieged* (New York: Basic Books, 1977); for many Americans, the family might be likened to an emotional gas station, where they drop by to tank up on affection before pulling out into social traffic once more.

30. MacIntyre, "Corporate Modernity and Moral Judgment," 124.

31. Thomas J. Peters and Robert H. Waterman, Jr., *In Search of Excellence: Lessons from America's Best-Run Companies* (New York: Warner Books, 1982), 323; emphasis added.

32. Deal and Kennedy, 16.

33. Ibid.

34. MacIntyre, "Corporate Modernity and Moral Judgment," 123.

35. Cf. Alasdair MacIntyre, *Against the Self-Images of the Age* (New York: Schocken Books, 1971), 123–24, 168–69.

36. Alasdair MacIntyre, *Whose Justice? Which Rationality?* (Notre Dame, IN: University of Notre Dame Press, 1988), 27–28.

37. Prof. Thomas J. C. Raymond with Elisabeth Ament Lipton, "Tylenol," *Harvard Business School Case* (Boston: President and Fellows of Harvard College, 1984), 1.

38. Ibid., 2–3.

39. Ibid., 4.

40. Ibid., 11.

41. Ibid., 10.

42. James E. Burke, "The Leverage of Goodwill," (speech to the Advertising Council, 16 November 1983), 4.

43. "Leadership of the Most Admired," *Fortune,* (29 January 1990), 50.

44. MacIntyre, *After Virtue,* 175.

45. Cf. Jeffrey Stout, *Ethics After Babel* (Boston: Beacon Press, 1988), 269. Speaking of medical practice in his article in this volume "We Are All Pragmatists Now: The Limits of Modern Medical Ethics in American Medical Education", Richard Vance has insightfully pointed out that *contra* Stout (and thus MacIntyre as well), there is not so wide or clear a gap between internal and external goods as we have been led to believe:

> Yet medicine as a craft has always, even in Hippocratic times, considered remuneration to be closely connected to the quality of care. Money and prestige are not, of course, direct goals of medical practice, but they are not merely external attachments either. One need not be a cynical critic of medicine to note that financial issues are more complexly related to medical practice than Stout's analysis admits (p. 50).

Vance's observation concerning medical practice obviously has implications for other kinds of practices as well.

46. MacIntyre, *After Virtue,* 175.

47. See above, fn. 4.

48. Trachtenberg and Foner, 5–6.

49. Bellah et al., 290.

50. St. Basil, *Ascetical Works,* trans. Sr. Monica M. Wagner, C.S.C. (New York: Fathers of the Church, Inc., 1950), xi; Armand Veilleux, trans. and

introduction, *The Life of Saint Pachomius and His Disciples,* foreword by Adalbert de Vogue, vol. 1, Cistercian Studies Series, no. 45 (Kalamazoo, MI: Cistercian Publications, Inc., 1980), xvii.

51. Lawrence M. Friedman, *A History of American Law,* 2nd ed. (New York: Simon & Schuster, 1985), 201.

52. Trachtenberg and Foner, 6.

53. Bryan Burrough and John Helyar, *Barbarians at the Gate: The Fall of RJR Nabisco* (New York: Harper & Row, 1990), 45, 49, 91, 511; emphasis added.

54. Burke, 3–4.

55. *Atlanta Journal Constitution,* (11 December 1989), sec. B, 6.

56. Phillips and Kennedy, 5.

57. Peters and Waterman, Jr., 292–93, and McKinsey & Co. research.

58. Raymond with Lipton, 10.

59. Maimonides, Mishneh Torah, Hilchot Yesodei HaTorah 5:3.

60. A failure to see this difference can result in the kind of business apologia written by Michael Novak; cf. his *Toward A Theology of the Corporation* (Washington, D.C.: American Enterprise Institute, 1981), and *The Spirit of Democratic Capitalism* (New York: Simon and Schuster, 1982).

We Are All Pragmatists Now: The Limits of Modern Medical Ethics in American Medical Education

Richard P. Vance, M.D.

Introduction

Robert Petersdorf, president of the Association of American Medical Colleges, is one of the most respected observers of the medical education scene. In 1988, he wrote about the problems facing medical education using the metaphor of Scylla and Charybdis.[1] He argued that teaching hospitals are torn between financial risk and social responsibility for indigent care; medical school faculties are forced to choose among the conflicting demands of clinical practice, research, and teaching; and medical students are forced to choose between the financial rewards of subspecialization and the social needs of primary care service. He concluded that we are not likely ever to find our way beyond these conflicts. The best we can do is to steer a course between conflicting sets of demands. What Petersdorf did not tell us, though, is what we should use as our rudder.

Clearly, this is no small criticism, since it is tantamount to suggesting that we lack not only a coherent goal for medical education but also a coherent criterion for assessing it. Indeed, Edmund Pellegrino has argued that despite all the interest in medical education reform, insufficient attention had been given to the ethical assessment of medical education.[2] One reason that such assessments have appeared so infrequently, I believe, is that they immediately uncover perennial and intractable dilemmas.

The rare attempts to provide a framework for evaluating medical educational goals bear this out. Such frameworks fall into two distinct patterns. The first is displayed most clearly by Carlos Martini.[3] He fully
acknowledges the sad reality that goals for medical education have been
far more difficult to determine than most of us want to admit. We even
lack coherent definitions of crucial concepts, such as clinical competence,
that underlie such goals. Martini is convinced, nevertheless, that all we
need to do to resolve our current difficulties is to provide more resources
and more cooperation. We must, he argues, redouble our efforts to experiment, innovate, analyze, invest, and study.[4,5]

Deborah Borek sees the issues differently.[6] She is weary of those who,
like Martini, constantly clamor for solutions. Indeed, seeking solutions,
she argues, is part of our problem. Medical education's problems are,
for Borek, merely intellectual. Problems in defining the proper kinds
of physicians who ought to be educated are, of course, troubling at a
theoretical level. But we shouldn't be too concerned because we are at
a practical level doing rather well. Physicians are, generally speaking,
morally upright and clinically competent. The lack of coherent definitions shouldn't bother us, therefore, because agreement on these issues is
extremely unlikely anyway.

Neither Martini nor Borek considers the possibility, however, that the
failures might be due to extraprofessional sources. In other words, they
don't consider medical education's problems to be primarily social or political. This essay will show why problems facing medical education are
directly related to broader problems in our liberal culture. It is far from
obvious, though, how one can connect such complex and disparate topics
as medical education, medical ethics, the institutional structure of modern medicine, and the dilemmas of Enlightenment democracy. Fortu-
nately, these relationships become much clearer through an examination
of the history of American medical education, particularly by focusing
on the unrivalled influence John Dewey has had on medical education.
Unlike Borek, therefore, I shall show that the problems besetting medical
education are not merely theoretical, but are embedded in all the practices we call medical. Unlike Martini, I shall suggest that we are not

likely to overcome significant moral problems in medical education simply by redoubling our current efforts.

Ethical Implications of the History of American Medical Education

Incorporation of Medical Education into American Universities

Success and power came to American universities almost a generation ahead of medical education.[7,8] Strong university presidents like Charles Eliot at Harvard actively pursued the incorporation of medical schools into the university.[9] Medical schools were in no position to resist during these initial reforms because they depended upon their parent university's subsidies to continue in operation. As a result, modern medical education came to take place within a complex, corporate, bureaucratic structure.[10] As Kenneth Ludmerer describes it,

> The fundamental insight into American medical practice today . . . is that it is changing in structure to accommodate the arrival of the corporation. The fundamental insight into American medical education, however, is that it is not changing in structure because by the 1920s it had already taken a corporate form. In the early twentieth century, the university medical school displaced the privately-owned proprietary schools, in a fashion analogous to the displacement of traditional private practice by corporate medicine today. Corporations . . . is [sic] what the university schools indeed are. With their huge plants, facilities, staffs, and financial resources, they could teach medicine employing numerous efficiencies of scale that no proprietary school could hope to match. In addition, they have adopted a corporate organizational structure. Medical schools are run by powerful executive "chiefs"—the department chairmen—whose enormous influence is matched only by their large degree of autonomy. Their role in the medical school is analogous to that of senior executives responsible for major divisions in large businesses. In the modern medical schools, as in the modern corporation, everyone is salaried. The rewards to employees— the full-time instructors—do not come directly from their contact with

patients but from academic promotions—a move up the corporate hierarchy. These observations explain the remarkable constancy of the medical school over the past sixty years, even as the content of medical education and the structure of medical practice have so dramatically changed.[11]

The principal effect of the corporate infrastructure for medical education was the narrowing of medical education to a single path. No competitors were permitted, either in medical philosophy or in educational method.

Emergence of Distinctive Medical Educational Philosophy

Ludmerer has shown convincingly that American medical educators began writing and speaking about a form of education in the 1870s that would eventually be associated with John Dewey's progressive education movement in the twentieth century. From the very beginnings of this early period of medical education reform, "the primary goal of medical education . . . was not to provide students an encyclopedic knowledge of facts but to foster the student's ability to think critically, to solve problems, to acquire new information, to keep up with the changing times.[12] The new educational philosophy had two important aspects, and both became central to Deweyan pragmatism: First, practical education involved "knowledge through doing it"; and second, the relationship between science and ethics was one of interdependence.

New Concepts of Knowledge and Action

As Dewey often argued, the true form of modern science leads us to recognize its inevitable applicability: "in a profound sense knowing ceases to be contemplative and becomes practical."[13] Hence, the physician, like the scientist, becomes an *intelligent artisan*. Knowledge is acquired in medicine through experience. Such experience forms habits that train the mind to understand the reality with which it is confronted:

> From the multitude of particular illnesses encountered, the physician in learning to class some of them as indigestion learns also to treat the cases of

the class in a common or general way. He forms the rule of recommending a certain diet, and prescribing a certain remedy. All this forms what we call experience. It results . . . in a certain general insight and a certain organized ability in action.[14]

The most direct reflection of this *craftsmanlike* perspective in medical education occurred at Johns Hopkins with the introduction of the clinical clerkship.[15] Previous clinical educational formats permitted medical students only to watch others examine patients. Clinical clerks were intimately and continuously involved in the care of patients. This innovation, introduced principally by William Osler, transformed the methods of clinical education.

> Under this system . . . the hospital became the medical school. . . . Under appropriate supervision, students took patients' histories, performed physical examinations, and carried out procedures such as examining the blood smear or urine, inserting catheters, and apply dressing changes. . . . In this way students obtained a first-hand knowledge of disease and clinical methods. The clerkship thus represented a pedagogic revolution of the first magnitude. It allowed the principle of learning by doing to be applied in the clinical subjects, as laboratory instruction had done in the scientific work.[16]

Well before Dewey, therefore, prominent medical educators such as John Shaw Billings, the intellectual architect of Johns Hopkins medical school, were extolling the value of this new pragmatic education: "An important part of the higher education of modern times is teaching how to increase knowledge; and the best way of teaching this, as of many other things, is by doing it, and by causing the pupils to do it."[17] Once Dewey's views became known, medical educators eagerly embraced them. Indeed, Abraham Flexner officially endorsed Dewey's educational goals, even as he reported that "the ideas of progressive education have permeated professional education."[18] Flexner, quoting Dewey, defined science as "as a method of thinking, an attitude of mind, after the pattern of which mental habits are to be transformed."[19] Flexner, therefore, solidified the connection between medicine's academic inclinations and Dewey's progressive education. Indeed, every reform initiative since

Flexner, including the General Professional Education of the Physician (GPEP) report and the most recent Robert Wood Johnson interim report, have sought to reemphasize the progressive presuppositions of medical education.[20]

Medical Conceptions of Science and Ethics

Just as medical education came to embody Deweyan notions of the relationship between knowledge and action, it also embraced the Deweyan understanding of the connection between science and ethics. Ethics, Dewey argued, "is not something with a separate province. It is physical, biological, and historic knowledge placed in a human context where it will illuminate and guide the activities of men."[21] Faulty notions of science are reductive, Dewey argued, because they create "a world of things indifferent to human interests."[22]

> When physics, chemistry, biology, medicine, contribute to the detection of concrete human woes and to the development of plans for remedying them and relieving the human estate, they become moral; they become part of the apparatus of moral inquiry or science.[23]

Hence, for Dewey, medicine and ethics are inextricably bound to one another. This perspective informed Richard Cabot, who noted in 1918 that medical education should provide the means for "the preparedness for treating a human being as if he possessed a mind, affections, talents, vices and habits good and bad, as well as more or less diseased organs."[24] Dewey's influence is just as clear in one of the most often quoted articles in medicine, Francis Peabody's 1927 article "The Care of the Patient":

> The practice of medicine in its broadest sense includes the whole relationship of the physician with his patient. It is an art, based to an increasing extent on the medical sciences, but comprising much that still remains outside the realm of any science. The art of medicine and the science of medicine are not antagonistic but supplementary to each other. There is no more contradiction between the science of medicine and the art of medicine than between the science of aeronautics and the art of flying. . . . One of the essential

qualities of the clinician is interest in humanity, for the secret of the care of the patient is in caring for the patient.[25]

Unlike the connection between knowledge and action, however, the Deweyan insight regarding science and ethics was submerged for a time under positivist paradigms. Only with the development of postpositivist conceptions of scientific rationality and the modern medical ethics movement has this Deweyan ethical perspective re-emerged.

Pragmatism in Modern Medical Ethics

The Inadequacies of Deweyan Pragmatism

Still, Ludmerer concludes his recent history of American medical education with the following assessment:

> For over a century, the goal of medical education has been to produce thinking physicians, scientifically competent, who are sensitive to the emotional as well as the medical condition of the patient. Medical educators in each successive generation have reaffirmed their belief in that ideal. The problem has not been the validity of the ideal but the great difficulty of achieving it in practice.[26]

Given what I have said so far, one might reasonably ask why there is a problem in medical education at all. If the practical and institutional aspects of medical education have remained consistent, and the ethical side of Deweyan medical practice is no longer subverted by positivism, why does defining the goals of medicine remain an intractable problem?

Two reasons are most obvious, I believe. First, medicine's problems are not simply internal to medical practice. Second, Dewey's optimistic liberalism is no longer plausible. The problems facing medicine and society, most would now agree, are more serious than Dewey imagined. Indeed, the most potent philosophical critics of liberalism are probably on to something. In particular, Alasdair MacIntyre's arguments about liberalism imply that it is impossible for us to construct a coherent philosophy or ethic for medical education.

MacIntyre has argued that the problems of modern liberalism are really problems *within* liberalism—problems embedded in the presuppositions that sustain our liberal culture.[27,28] Most of his criticisms intend to show that all post-Enlightenment positions have failed, and that they must fail, precisely because they ignore their own historical, tradition-bound character. It is our profoundest myth, MacIntyre argues, that we have created a society in which rational, autonomous individuals can live peacefully in the midst of a plurality of moral perspectives. In turn, we inhabit a culture characterized by incommensurable fragments of moral traditions.

> For what many of us are educated into is, not a coherent way of thinking and judging, but one constructed out of an amalgam of social and cultural fragments inherited both from different traditions from which our culture was originally derived (Puritan, Catholic, Jewish) and from different stages in and aspects of the development of modernity. . . . [29]

These intellectual fragments, moreover, were "originally at home in larger totalities of theory and practice in which they enjoyed a role and function supplied by contexts of which they have now been deprived."[30] Hence,

> The surface rhetoric of our culture is apt to speak complacently of moral pluralism in this connection, but the notion of pluralism is too imprecise. For it may equally well apply to an ordered dialogue of intersecting viewpoints and to an unharmonious melange of ill-assorted fragments.[31]

MacIntyre's criticisms ring true to many of us and make the optimistic pragmatism of Dewey seem incredibly naive. To "act in the patient's best interest" might provide substantive moral guidance in the midst of a coherent moral tradition. It seems to be little more than an empty platitude in a culture that can embrace both Rawlsian and Nozickean theories of justice, and where the notions of Jack Kervorkian, Derek Humphrey, Leon Kass, and Edmund Pellegrino toward physician responsibility to dying patients are equally at home.

Jeffrey Stout's Stereoscopic Social Criticism

However, in response to MacIntyre's criticisms, a more recent pragmatist option has emerged. Jeffrey Stout, using in part Davidson's famous article on the logical impossibility of distinct conceptual schemes, has argued that disagreements in our society are not as complete as MacIntyre has proposed.[32] Indeed, if they were total disagreements, they would be merely *verbal,* for we would be arguing about different subjects.

> Even though we no longer share a single theory of human nature (when did we exactly?) and despite the fact that Aristotelian teleology has long since passed out of philosophical fashion, most of us do agree on the essentials of what might be called the provisional telos of our society. What made the creation of liberal institutions necessary, in large part, was the manifest failure of religious groups of various sorts to establish rational agreement on their competing detailed visions of the good. . . . In other words, certain features of our society can be seen as justified by a self-limiting consensus on the good—an agreement consisting partly in the realization that it would be a bad thing, that it would make life worse for us all, to press too hard or too far for agreement on all details in a given vision of the good. We can define our shared conceptions of the good as the set of all platitudinous judgments employing such terms as good, better than, and the like. We can define a platitude . . . as a judgment that only the philosophers (and the morally incompetent or utterly vicious) among us would think of denying.[33]

Stout's argument is that MacIntyre has aimed his critical arguments at the wrong target. The foundationalist arguments for liberal democracy are indeed dead, Stout would maintain. Yet the liberal tradition, as interpreted by pragmatists, never needed those arguments anyway. MacIntyre has defeated only the weakest defenders of liberal democracy, not liberalism itself.

For Stout, we do lack the fully constitutive notion of community that Dewey was interested in constructing.[34]

> Our society and its distinctive modes of public discourse are best viewed . . . as the result of a manifest failure to achieve agreement on a fully

detailed conception of the good—as the arrangements and conventions of people who contracted, in effect, to limit the damage of that failure by settling for a thinner conception of the good that more people could agree to, given the alternatives and until something better comes along.[35]

We do not need, therefore, a pre-Enlightenment community in order to have a tolerable society. Provisional agreement for the sake of nonviolent coexistence is all that is necessary. What liberal democracy loses in profundity, Stout argues, it gains in tolerance.

This careful balancing act is extended to Stout's analysis of our social institutions. For example, when he turns to medicine, Stout provides what he calls a *stereoscopic social criticism*. Modern medicine is best viewed, Stout argues, from two perspectives at the same time: as a *social practice*, and as an *institution*. Borrowing from MacIntyre's own arguments, Stout presents medicine first as an example of a social practice, by which he means:

> any coherent and complex form of socially established cooperative human activity through which goods internal to that form of activity are realized in the course of trying to achieve those standards of excellence which are appropriate to, and partially definitive of, that form of activity, with the result that human powers to achieve excellence, and human conceptions of the ends and goods involved, are systematically extended.[36]

Hence, social practices like medicine display *internal goods,* those goods that are intrinsic parts of an activity (i.e. such as practicing medicine or playing chess well).

> Doctors and nurses pursue goods internal to the practice of medical care, goods that cannot be achieved in any other practice or by any other means than by being a good doctor or nurse, acquiring and exhibiting the qualities, forms of excellence, or virtues peculiar to those roles. . . . It requires the cultivation of qualities that might be called the cardinal virtues of medicine . . . practical wisdom, the ability to exercise sound medical judgment and discernment; justice, the capacity to give everyone involved

in or affected by the practice their due. . . . ; courage, the strength of character required to risk danger . . . ; temperance, a trait that keeps one pursuing goods internal to the practice. . . . [37]

Such a social practice, Stout believes, displays numerous relatively uncon-
troversial good ends.

> We want our doctors and nurses to care for us when we are sick, to ease our
> suffering and cure us when they can, to inform us about how to prevent
> illness, to learn whatever they need to learn to do all of these things, and to
> receive just monetary compensations and prestige (no more, no less) in re-
> turn. We are prepared, if at times reluctantly, to submit to their authority,
> to put our lives in their hands, even when they are strangers to us. Despite
> our concerns about their fallibility, the corruptions of prestige and wealth,
> and the facelessness of modern medical bureaucracies, we still pay tribute to
> the virtues and worth of medical practitioners. Few of them are saints, but
> most are more than technicians. Most of the cases they treat in our hospitals
> and clinics raise no serious moral problems for us.[38]

Medicine displays concretely, therefore, the primacy of social practice in
our liberal democracy. Social practices are our first language, Stout argues; individualism is nothing more than our language of last resort.[39]
Hence, we already have in our social practices the most important moral
resources MacIntyre says we need for a healthy society.

However, Stout continues, medicine is also composed of an *institutional
structure,* the bureaucratic corporate structure of academic medicine.
Here, unlike social practices, *external goods* such as money, power, prestige
are preeminent.

> In our society the practice of medical care is embodied in institutions such as
> professional associations, medical schools, partnerships, independent hospi-
> tals, and increasingly powerful commercial hospital chains. . . . Institutions
> typically pose significant moral threats to the social practices they make possi-
> ble. Goods like money and power and status, which have no internal relation
> to a social practice like medical care, can compete with and even engulf goods
> internal to the practice.[40]

Our task as ethicists is to use the dual perspectives of social practice and institutional structure to preserve internal goods. We cannot do that without institutions, yet those same institutions provide a constant threat to the internal goods. Hence, our task is to balance these mutually dependent but distinct elements in our moral lives.

Stout presents us, therefore, with a chastened version of pragmatism that claims to have overcome the overly optimistic implications of Dewey's position by ruling out the need for a strong sense of community in liberal life. Stout claims, therefore, to have taken full advantage of what we have learned from the mistakes and failures of analytical and foundationalist philosophies, as well as the social disruptions of late twentieth-century liberalism.

The Educational Limits of Pragmatism

Given what I have said so far, one might legitimately ask again why my subtitle refers to the limits of medical ethics in medical education. Indeed, it would seem that Stout has provided precisely the postmodern pragmatism needed to address Petersdorf's intractable problems. However, the situation is not so simple for many reasons. Indeed, I believe Stout's two-part social ethic inadequately describes the nature and the interaction between practice and institution in modern medicine. Just how serious my reservations are becomes clear by examining each aspect (practice and institution) separately.

Medicine as a Social Practice

Even if all we need is consensus on provisional ends, modern medicine presents us with significant problems. In order to have even marginal agreement on goals, we must also have at least provisional agreement on the criteria for deciding how conflicts between such platitudinous goals are to be resolved. And as MacIntyre points out, unresolvable conflicts of this sort are pervasive in modern medicine.

> To put matters oversimply: from Hippocrates until almost the present the three ends of medical practice were highly congruent with each other. To

pursue any one of the three generally involved pursuing the other two also. What were those three ends? First to stave off the patient's death for as long as possible; secondly to prevent the patient's suffering pain or physical disability as far as possible; and thirdly to promote the patient's general health and physical well-being. . . . But with contemporary medicine these ends fall apart. The chronic conditions which require treatment and the technology available as the instrument of treatment allows us to continue life in such a way as to prolong suffering or to extend disability. There may be no way to promote my well-being which does not involve bringing about my death at a certain point; it may even be better for me if I had not been born. The physician or surgeon, therefore, pledged by his oath and the tradition of his profession to pursue all three ends now is forced, especially with the chronic conditions, to make choices, choices sufficiently frequent in occurrence and sufficiently harsh in character for moral choice to have become a central medical task.[41]

How are we then, in the presence of these conflicts, to train physicians to be *good* physicians? How can the virtues of the good physician ever be more than sentimental ideals hiding essentially arbitrary decisions? Indeed, don't we find that medical education is *already* dominated by the strong personality and the effective speaker? It is no accident that most physicians practice in ways consistent with their most influential mentors. The strong rhetorician, the master craftsman remain the most powerful educational elements in medicine. The platitudinous goals of medicine come to mean, therefore, simply what particularly strong physicians *choose* for them to mean.

Just as important, specialization fragments the goals of medical practice both for practitioners and for patients. Geneticists, surgeons, and psychiatrists come to similar patients with very different presuppositions about the meaning of *the patient's best interests*. Patients perceive this fragmentation as well.

The patient may not see the doctor even during the same illness on any two successive occasions; different doctors attend to different members of the family and to different parts of the body. . . . The modern patient therefore approaches the physician as stranger to stranger; and the very proper fear and suspicion that we have of strangers extends equally properly to our encounter with physicians. We do not and cannot know what to expect of them. This situation is met in medicine as elsewhere by supplying organizational guarantees.[42]

Medicine as an Institutional Structure

Indeed, when we turn to medicine as an institution, Stout's problems only increase, because the bureaucratic mechanisms in medicine turn out to be much more than a force external to medical practice.[43]

> Problems of medical ethics . . . are secondary to problems of medical organization; and problems of medical organization turn out to have a crucial moral dimension. For insofar as choices between forms of organization have implications for role definition, they at least partially determine moral problems we will encounter.[44]

The most obvious example is in medical economics. Stout's analysis classifies economic matters as external goods in medicine. Yet medicine as a craft has always, even in Hippocratic times, considered remuneration to be closely connected to the quality of care. Money and prestige are not, of course, direct goals of medical practice, but they are not merely external attachments either. One need not be a cynical critic of medicine to note that financial issues are more complexly related to medical practice than Stout's analysis admits.

In our society, financial structures in health care are construed to produce certain goals. The private sector hopes to make a profit; the public sector tries to distribute limited goods and services. Both of these financial sources often provide incentives to treat patients less than optimally. What sort of financial incentives, then, if any, should physicians endure, or be trained to endure? To suggest that physicians should be protected from the financial consequences of their decisions, or that there should be no incentives for fiscal constraint would be incredibly naive and/or socially irresponsible. But what kind of incentives *should* there be? Fee-for-service encourages physicians to do as much as they can for each patient. Yet such a system encourages enormous expenditures of social resources.

Indeed, the absence of a substantive consensus on such issues of justice leaves the medical profession with pervasive conflicts between financial incentives and patient welfare. How can a pragmatist ethic lead a physician to balance the good of an individual patient against the common good, or even against the good of a medical corporation? Here pragmatist platitudes offer no consistent guidance. Pragmatists can only hope the conflicts do not become too serious.

Stout's use of MacIntyre's distinctions between social practice and institutional structure, therefore, turn out to distort the nature of modern medicine because Stout interprets the distinction too simply and too starkly. Medicine's social practice and institutional structure are much more closely and complexly connected. Institutional structures are not merely the vessels within which the social practices of medicine take place. Indeed, social practices are virtually nothing more than enactment of bureaucratic rules that constitute our institutions. Stout's stereoscopic social criticism, at least as he applies it to medicine, serves only to hypostatize two abstract perspectives of a very complex social institution.

Conclusions

In the fourth century B.C.E., a group of physicians in Thebes decided to commit to writing those moral convictions that described the nature of their life together. Their product, the Hippocratic Oath, included affirmations of Hellenic deities, kinship ties, obligations and virtues of their practice, and their vision of the proper ends of human life. The Oath was an unusual document for that period of history because it demanded behavior more strict than was commonplace. These physicians considered medicine to be the "greatest wisdom attainable by men"; it was for them fundamentally a noble practice, a practice worthy of honor.

We seldom acknowledge, though, that the Hippocratic Oath makes sense as an historical document only because the fraternity it described no longer existed.[45] Indeed, the Oath was written by Pythagoreans who found their sect not only disbanded, but also struggling to exist in a foreign milieu. In the absence of social and political support, Pythagorean physicians were reduced to stating in abbreviated and abstract form those common values, obligations, and goals constitutive of their community. Yet in thus articulating their most important convictions, the authors displayed why those same convictions had become more like platitudes than lived practices. When it becomes necessary to write down our life goals, living the sort of life that would allow us to attain those goals has become difficult indeed.

In this respect, most of modern medical ethics resembles the Hippocratic Oath, not because it defends Pythagorean values, but because it ignores the dominant social and political features of modern medicine. For this reason, medical ethicists should be distinguished not so much by whether they are duty-based or virtue-based theorists, but by whether they recognize the way in which modern bureaucracy controls and defines medicine's ethic. Regulation, as MacIntyre puts it, has become our dominant morality.[46] When medical ethicists ignore this bureaucratic ethos, they resemble Pythagorean oath-makers longing for an ethic that has long-since passed out of existence.

Where does such a view of modern medicine lead us? We are left with the utter absence of a coherent ethic for medicine except in so far as bureaucratic mechanisms maintain medicine's platitudinous language. The good news is that by recognizing this vacuum physicians might begin to be educated about the moral limits in our liberal democracy, and the interminable character of medicine's problems. Petersdorf was, after all, correct. The problems facing medical education will not go away, because those problems reflect the limits of medical ethics in medical education, and the limits of any ethic in a liberal culture. Recognizing these limits is a start.

The bad news is that in such a recognition, physicians will quickly learn that for ethical resources they have nothing more to call upon than those procedural guides embodied in statutory and case law. The sobering result is that our best American *physicians*—in the absence of substantive moral alternatives—will begin to look very much like American *lawyers*.

NOTES

1. Robert Petersdorf, "The Scylla and Charybdis of Medical Education," *J Med Educ* 63 (1988), 88–93.

2. Edmund Pellegrino, "Medical Education," in *Encyclopedia of Bioethics,* ed. W. T. Reich, et al (New York: Free Press, 1978), 863.

3. Carlos Martini, "The Long Shadow of Flexner: A Prolonged Polemic in Assessing Outcomes in Medical Education," *JAMA* 262 (1989), 1008–1010.

4. Ibid.

5. E. J. Stemmler, "Medical Education: Is it?" *J Med Educ* 63 (1988), 81–87.

6. Deborah Borek, "Unchanging Dilemmas in American Medical Education," *Acad Med* 64 (1989), 240–244.

7. K. M. Ludmerer, *Learning to Heal: The Development of American Medical Education* (New York: Basic Books, 1985), 38.

8. B. J. Bledstein, *The Culture of Professionalism* (New York: Norton, 1976).

9. Ludmerer, *Learning to Heal,* 48–50.

10. Ibid., 268.

11. Ibid., 276.

12. Ibid., 52.

13. John Dewey, *Reconstruction in Philosophy* (Boston: Beacon Press, 1957), 116.

14. Ibid., 80.

15. Ludmerer, *Learning to Heal,* 60.

16. Ibid., 60.

17. Ibid., 64.

18. Ibid., 167.

19. Ibid., 176.

20. C. Enarson, "Previous Reform Initiatives in Medical Education" (Prepared for the Robert Wood Johnson Commission on Medical Education, 1991).

21. John Dewey, *The Quest for Certainty* (1929). Quoted by Mary Warnock, *Ethics Since 1900* (London: Oxford, 1960), 77.

22. John Dewey, *The Public and Its Problems* (Chicago: Swallow, 1927), 173–78.

23. Dewey, *Reconstruction in Philosophy,* 173.

24. R. C. Cabot, *Training and Rewards of the Physician* (Philadelphia: Lippincott, 1918), 42.

25. Francis Peabody, "The Care of the Patient," *JAMA* 88 (1927), 887–892.

26. Ludmerer, *Learning to Heal,* 277–78.

27. Alasdair MacIntyre, *After Virtue,* 2nd ed. (Notre Dame, IN: University of Notre Dame Press, 1984).

28. Alasdair MacIntyre, *Whose Justice? Which Rationality?* (Notre Dame, IN: University of Notre Dame Press, 1988).

29. Ibid., 2.

30. MacIntyre, *After Virtue,* 10.

31. Ibid.

32. Jeffrey Stout, *Ethics After Babel* (Boston: Beacon Press, 1988).

33. Ibid., 212–13.

34. R. Bernstein "John Dewey on Democracy: The Task Before Us," *Philosophical Profiles* (Philadelphia: University of Pennsylvania Press, 1986), 260–72.

35. Stout, *Ethics After Babel,* 225.

36. MacIntyre, *After Virtue,* 187.

37. Stout, *Ethics After Babel,* 269.

38. Ibid., 281–82.

39. Ibid., 271.

40. Ibid., 274.

41. Alasdair MacIntyre, "What has Ethics to Learn from Medical Ethics?," *Philosophic Exchange* 2 (1978), 37–47.

42. Alasdair MacIntyre, "Patients as Agents," in *Philosophical Medical Ethics* (Boston: D. Reidel, 1977), 206–7.

43. Alasdair MacIntyre, "Medicine Aimed at the Care of Persons Rather Than What . . . ?"

44. MacIntyre, "What has Ethics to Learn," 46.

45. L. Edelstein, "The Hippocratic Oath," O. Temkin and C. Temkin, *Ancient Medicine* (Baltimore: Johns Hopkins Press, 1967).

46. Alasdair MacIntyre, "Regulation: A Substitute for Morality," *Hastings Center Report* 10 (February 1980), 31–33.

The Valued Therapist

Deborah Fernhoff

The owner of a kosher restaurant in Teaneck, New Jersey had been tremendously successful and wanted to expand his business to a store across the street. His four competitors on the same street petitioned a specially convened *bet din* (rabbinical court) to stop this expansion on the principle of *hasagat gvul* (overstepping boundaries). The other owners charged that if he were to expand, he would draw business away from their restaurants and jeopardize their livelihoods. The rabbinical authorities of the *bet din* will hear the case to make a decision about the expansion. If they rule against it, and the owner refuses to comply, they can revoke his kosher certification. Rabbi Neil Winkler of the Fort Lee Young Israel comments, "We are not only concerned that what you put in your mouth is kosher, but that your business ethics must be properly kosher as well."

At the time of this writing, the *bet din* has not yet decided. The responses of typical Americans to this concept are fascinating: "What do you mean a business owner can't expand his business when he wants to? If other businesses fail, then they just weren't competitive enough." We operate by the free enterprise system which reinforces an individual's energy, expertise, and business acumen. The principle of *hasagat gvul* emphasizes the needs of the community to maintain enough *parnasah* (livelihood) for as many members as possible; as some wags hold about the stock market, "you can be a bull or a bear but not a pig." The *bet din* will meet to decide how the Teaneck community of owners and customers can best be met. This is not an issue of law within the American legal system, but of ethics within an Orthodox Jewish frame.

The Ethical Framework of the Psychotherapist

Psychotherapists operate within the ethical frames of their specialities. Psychologists, psychiatrists, social workers, family therapists, and counselors have designated rules for what constitutes ethical behavior. However, to be honest, the majority of ethical standards are couched to avoid malpractice liability. Many of these ethics are common-sense applications of the basic maxim to "do no harm." Most of the injunctions are in the "thou shalt not" category: thou shalt not divulge confidentiality, thou shalt not engage in sexual behavior with patients, thou shalt not fail to warn a potential victim if your patient threatens harm. What, then, are the "shalts," the guiding principles that psychotherapists follow in treating their patients? The meta-ethics of the psychotherapeutic encounter are grounded within the values-set of the individual psychotherapist. Definitions of mental health vary based on the values-frame of the definer, as shown by the following two definitions:

> Ben Zoma said, Who is wise? He who learns from all men; as it is said, From all my teachers I have gotten understanding. Who is mighty? He who subdues his passions; as it is said, He that is slow to anger is better than the mighty, and he that ruleth over his spirit than he that taketh a city. Who is rich? He who rejoices in his portion; as it is said, When thou eatest the labour of thine hands, happy art thou, and it shall be well with thee; happy art thou in this world; and it shall be well with thee in the world to come. Who is worthy of honor? He who respects his fellow men; as it is said, For them that honor me I will honor and they that despise me shall be held in contempt. (Pirke Avos, IV:1)

Who is mentally healthy? The definition commonly understood within the field is that it is one who is self-aware, independent, able to cope, assertive, not conflicted or inhibited, and who enjoys and is satisfied with life. The mentally healthy person has self esteem, is confident, and autonomous; and is not neurotic.

This definition for emotional health delineates the goals of psychotherapy. In the section from Pirke Avos, the questions and answers hinge on the person's relationship to other people. Wisdom is not conferred by a Ph.D; it is based on an openness to others; the wise man is willing to learn from anybody. Might is not conferred by expertise in akido or pumping iron; self-conquest of one's own evil inclination constitutes strength. Wealth is measured through integrity and happiness in one's life work. Honor is based less on individual achievements and status than on maintaining ethical behavior toward others.

L. D. Hankoff, writing in the *Proceedings of the Associations of Orthodox Jewish Scientists,* notes that the values of psychotherapy are a reflection of the values of society. Although Thomas Szasz has argued that psychotherapy can be a form of social control, psychotherapists do not necessarily merely adjust an individual to society. Psychotherapists are as much a part of a society and its values as patients; both parties often operate within the same *zeitgeist*. This is especially true when psychotherapy has been freely chosen by the patient and is not mandated by the state (as was the role of psychiatrists in the former U.S.S.R.) or court system (for child custody, return of driver's license following a conviction for driving under the influence of alcohol, juvenile delinquency, etc.). In our own era, psychological findings and related values have had a tremendous impact on child rearing, marital and other interpersonal relationships, and the assessment and definition of a person's character.

Rather than biographies, we have psychohistories. We have less emphasis on the morally bad and good and more on the mentally sick and well. Psychodynamic and behavioral paradigms have had an impact on the culture, and in chicken-and-egg fashion, the culture creates and underwrites psychotherapy values.

Myths of Our Time

When the Beatles sang that we all live in a yellow submarine, whether they realized it or not that yellow submarine was the culture, society, and time frame that we inhabit. Both patient and therapist share a *zeitgeist,* or in Rollo May's words, dwell within the same set of myths. In *The Cry for*

Myth, May views the myth as a way of making sense in a senseless world: "Myths are narrative patterns that give significances to our existence." They are the narrative stories that tie together our society. Within the multiplicity of myths within a culture, a chosen few contain more power and claim more believers. A person does not have to be conscious of his or her personal myth in order to follow it. Eric Berne, working from within the transactional analysis model, touched on this notion with *Games People Play.* However, his book focused on psychopathology, on the defenses we engage to protect our anxiety and refuse life responsibility. His cute titles ("Uproar," "Blemish," and "Look How Hard I've Tried") were amusing and like the Audubon Guide to Birds became a kind of psychological parlor game for spotting deviance.

A myth, however, is bigger than a game. Rollo May's myth is similar to Alfred Adler's "guiding fiction," the story one tells about oneself to oneself through the years. If a person has internalized the story of David and Goliath, then he or she is willing to take on incredible odds for the sake of conviction. In the same vein, children still learn the story of *The Little Train that Could* in preschool to remember to keep trying even when the going is tough. The Horatio Alger myth has had a significant place in our history: poor boy, through his fine character and his industry, makes good. The work ethic and the democratic ideal both find credence within this myth. Our current era has made another myth central: the Lone Ranger, sans Tonto. The Lone Ranger rides alone and no one really knows who he is. He comes into town, performs a few heroic deeds, interacts briefly with the citizenry, and then he's off again. No family, no friends, no fixed address.

May presents the myth of Narcissus as the core myth of our time. Narcissus fell into unrequited love with his own reflection in a pool, and pined sadly away until he died.

Christopher Lasch saw us as a culture of narcissism: insecure, needing the approval of others desperately, frantically pursuing intense emotional experiences to feel something within the inner void, full of suppressed rage, and estranged from broader values that could give life meaning and make aging and death more acceptable.

According to Lasch, the narcissistic personality has become the dominant type of patient in America since the 1960s. The narcissist is sad, lonely, and shallow; the type of person who knows the price of every-thing and the value of nothing. The narcissist is self-indulgent and self-centered to the max. Narcissists are so full of self that they are emotionally empty. The paradox is that "therapy, for a number of rea-sons, some financial, some theoretical, and some simply an outgrowth of the behavioristic trends in our traditional American psychology, moves toward narcissism and excessive individualism, each empowering the other. Our psychotherapy then tends to be problem-centered rather than person-centered (p.114)."

Wallach and Wallach, writing in 1983, are highly critical of psy-chology's role in promulgating self as the ultimate good. They use the number of "pop psych" books on assertiveness as examples of this trend. If self-good is the highest value, then everyone is equal and whatever feels right is right (unless it interferes with someone else's space); there is no higher good. Personal gratification is the goal of proper adjustment. If a person suppresses desires, feelings, or thoughts, psychological distress or illness will ensue. Interestingly, research by the National Institutes for Mental Health shows that rates of depression in our society have increased to ten times what they were two generations ago (Buie, 1988). Martin Seligman attributes this finding to the in-creased emphasis on the self. Americans no longer have traditional broad sources of meaning and value in life, such as being part of a soci-ety or a religion. More, then, is demanded of the self: "It's the same as if some idiot raised the ante on what it takes to be a normal human being (p.52)."

Although psychotherapists have traditionally worked with sickness, whether within the individual (Freud) or within the society (Marcuse), we are increasingly being called on to work for "wellness." Both in the media and in public institutions, psychotherapists are asked to de-fine "health," moving from descriptive endeavors to prescriptive goals.

The Role of the Psychotherapist

One summer morning a few years ago, I saw four different patients in a row: 1) a young pre-medical student unsure of what he wanted to pur-sue within the medical field; 2) a Protestant bishop who had failed to move up farther in the clergy hierarchy; 3) a rabbi who struggled with depression and what to do with his future; and 4) a striptease dancer whose mind and body were tiring of her trade. If the specific content of each of these sessions were removed, each session could have been the other's replica. All four people were struggling with the twin issues of meaning and identity. Although the presenting problems differed and the intensity of feelings varied, all four were wrestling with making a meaningful place for themselves in their worlds and creating worthwhile self identities. Each was looking to the psychotherapeutic process to help find the path.

Roy Baumeister reviews the meanings of life in his book by that name. He concludes that in order for life to have meaning four needs must be met: purpose, value, efficacy, and self-worth. When people are told to "go for it," they have to have an "it" to go for. Both short-term and long-term goals structure a person's life and give direction. Values provide standards against which to judge the right or wrong of one's behavior. Neither as individuals nor as civilizations can we survive within a moral vacuum; values protect the individual from the group and the group from the individual.

Efficacy is the belief (not necessarily the fact) that we have control over our lives, that we can make a difference. Ongoing lack of a sense of control is a sure fire recipe for depression. Ironically, clinging to efficacy as a source of meaning can also generate depression. A seventy-five-year-old man who has always been the household manager, planner, and all-around "in charge person" insists on blaming himself for his seventy-two-year-old wife's heart attack and subsequent death. Even though there was nothing that he could have done to prevent the cardiac arrest or her death, he would rather hold on to his guilt than acknowledge a lack of efficacy.

Self-worth is involved with having self respect and the respect of others. (There is a faint echo in Baumeister's four with Ben Zoma's four; both pertain to how a person lives a meaningful life in relation to others.) Baumeister concludes that we have a values gap in the United States. The other three needs (purpose, efficacy, self-worth) have a number of avenues for fulfillment. We have elevated the glorification of self into a major value, to the detriment of family and community. Selfhood becomes a form of idolatry; the guiding ethos is "if it feels good, do it." Self-gratification provides justification for how one should act; looking out for number one is the primary rule. This narcissistic backdrop is the cultural stage upon which both therapist and patients play their roles.

What Does the Therapist Do?

In the personal history that each of us writes, we all start with chapter 2. The preface, introduction, and chapter 1 are written for us by the family, community, nation, and era into which we are born. However, the inherent notion in psychotherapy is that we have free will and we can then continue through our choices to write the rest.

The role of the psychotherapist is to help the patient determine what the guiding myth has been, decide if that is the one he or she wants to live, and then write his or her own story. The therapist is coach, editor, and sometimes critic for the budding novelist. Although others have shown the importance of the therapists' values for the patient, it is clear within the metaphor of writing one's own life story that the therapists' values impact strongly on the patient's choice of "myth" or life story. Within these cultural boundaries, what values or myths does the therapist select when guiding a patient's personal myth or life story? What are the values, from culture and from self, that the therapist brings into the therapy session?

The narcissistic culture finds its voice in a poem by Fritz Perls, the founder of Gestalt psychotherapy:

> I do my thing and you do your thing.
> I am not in this world to live up to your expectations,
> And you are not in this world to live up to mine.
> You are you and I am I.
> If by chance we find each other, it's beautiful.
> If not, it can't be helped.

When I first read this as a young graduate student, my compatriots and I saw this as permission to pursue our desires without worry or concern about anyone else. "Shoulds" and "oughts" were anathema. Perhaps, especially for women coming out of a restricted, "you should be good" era, this message had a freeing component. When I read it now as a middle-aged person, I am aghast. This is a paean to narcissism, to disconnection, to a lack of responsibility to others. I cannot imagine saying this to my family, friends, community, or patients. I do have expectations of myself and others; these are part of the social web we live within.

Can a husband say this to a wife? A parent to a child? A therapist to a patient?

What *should* the values be for psychotherapy? Perhaps we can find answers from other fields that address values, namely the fields of morality and religion.

E. Mansell Pattison wrote that the psychotherapist is a social change agent, particularly when the therapist and patient share the same set of values.

> The goal of the therapist is to enhance the patient's capabilities to deal with his society rather than merely to make the patient conform to society. (p. 109)

The therapist is hired to help the patient live a moral life as defined by the society to which both belong.

> In summary, to say that morality is a central concern of psychotherapy means that psychotherapy is ultimately aimed at clarifying the values to which the patient is committed, defining the values by which the patient wishes to pattern his life, and enabling the patient to synchronize his actual behavior with his goals and values. (p.110)

Although shallow, narcissistic values exist within a culture, other values cohabit the same time frame. Scott Peck's *The Road Less Traveled* has been an unlikely best-seller. This book by a psychiatrist opens with chapters on discipline and delaying gratification. Rabbi Harold Kushner's *When All You Ever Wanted Isn't Enough* was a New York Times best-seller for twenty-four weeks. This "self-help" book makes use of Ecclesiastes as the *myth* for modern times, the story of the man who has everything and feels nothing. Both of these books make strong cases for the strength of traditional religious values in defining a person's life.

The Relationship between
Psychotherapy and Religion?

At times, psychotherapy and religion have functioned best in two separate universes. When people were attached to their own synagogues and churches, they rarely seemed to bring issues of their spirituality into therapy. Psychotherapists probably did little to encourage such discussions; findings are that psychotherapists have a low rate of religious observance with psychologists reporting the lowest rates of all (Ragan, Malony, and Beit-Hallahmi, 1980). Attitudes toward patients' religious practices have varied from neutral to opprobrium. For example, my sister, in a court-ordered joint custody arrangement in New York City met with a court-appointed psychiatrist. The middle-aged psychiatrist exhorted her not to send her four-year-old son to an Orthodox Jewish preschool, saying that although the psychiatrist had himself grown up in a Jewish family, he could not wait to "shed himself" of his Jewishness and that she would do her son a disservice in life by not allowing him to do the same.

Religious groups have been wary, perhaps rightly so, of psychotherapy and psychotherapists, fearing that their teachings would be subverted. The late Rabbi Moshe Feinstein, who was the leading orthodox authority of this generation, issued two *halakhic responsa* in 1973 pertaining to the choice of competent practitioners of medicine and psychotherapy. When choosing a physician, the patient is enjoined to choose the more expert physician, even if he is an atheist. However, for the therapist, whose treatment involves words, an irreligious or agnostic practitioner may give advice contrary to religious law and should be avoided. A fundamental organizing principle for feminists has been to seek feminist psychotherapists, understanding that choosing a person not in congruence with shared goals was antithetical to positive emotional growth and change for women. *Newsweek* (9/14/92) reports on Christian therapy which utilizes traditional psychotherapeutic methods

within a Christian context. Of course there is a danger of a psychotherapeutic Balkanization, where therapy can strengthen stereotypes and
promote intolerance of others' beliefs. However, the alternative of a
parve (neither milk nor meat; in kosher terms, dietetically neutral) psychotherapy, is so watered down as to be useless to the patient in a quest
for a meaningful life.

I suspect that these issues will come even more to the fore as
managed care encompasses more of people's health care options. The
focus of managed care, generally speaking, is on rapid symptom relief.
At times, this can be accomplished with cognitive therapies, behavior
therapies, and/or medication. Here the focus is on the technique, not
on the practitioner. However, there will continue to be situations
where the problem lies within a patient's search for a meaningful life,
where the psychotherapeutic technique is less important than the person
of the therapist. Health insurance companies and managed care companies are entitled to ask if these issues are health-related [for which they
pay] or philosophy-related [for which they do not]. To which category
can be ascribed emotional conditions which have their roots in issues of
meaning?

L. D. Hankoff sees an inherent conflict between religion and evoca-
tive (based on the patient's history) therapies. Both psychotherapy and
religion offer total and comprehensive views of self and existence. In
psychotherapy, the ultimate goal is self-actualization through individual growth. The object in religion is to transcend the self and attain
grace through spiritual acts. Self is subservient to a greater good. Hankoff lists the possibilities of iatrogenic risk as a result of successful psychotherapy: 1) guilt may be absolved to a disproportionate degree; 2)
self-interest may crush altruism; 3) labeling past history as damaging
destroys a sense of pride and attachment to one's heritage; 4) the patient's previously loved family and friends become the enemy. Hankoff
feared that guilt would get explained away as neurotic symptomatology
rather than a person taking responsibility for the guilt-inducing behavior and making amends, through compensation, restitution, or apology.

For the sake of simplicity, we can divide therapy into three parts: the
therapist, the therapeutic interaction, and the patient.

When Freud introduced psychoanalysis, the therapist's task was to be a blank slate on which the patient projected dreams, fantasies, or desires. What the therapist brought in with him (not usually her) to the session was called countertransference, which a good analysis of the therapist could reduce if not eliminate. The psychotherapeutic process was the uncovering of the unconscious; the main focus of the therapy was on the patient. In the following years, a number of new therapies were introduced, most focusing on what happened in the therapy session. The techniques of client-centered, behavior, family, transactional analysis, cognitive, and other therapies all gave the patient and therapist something rather specific to do. An eclectic therapist carried a grab bag of different approaches to pull out as the occasion demanded.

In 1950 Freida Fromm-Reichman wrote that although a psychotherapist should be free in the analytic session from those values which pertain to religion, philosophy, or political viewpoints, there was an inherent set of values associated with psychoanalysis; namely, to help the patient become more self-understanding and freer from past irrational patterns in order to function more effectively. Carl Rogers also wanted to separate values from therapy:

> As therapy progresses, the client comes to realize that he is trying to live by what others think. But if he is to relinquish these introjected values, what is to take their place? There ensues a period of confusion and uncertainty as to values. Gradually this confusion is replaced by a dawning realization that the evidence upon which he can base a value judgement is supplied by his own senses, his own experience. (pp.149–150)

It is important to note that Rogers wrote this in 1951, within the *zeitgeist* of that era. The world had just endured the horrors of "orders are orders," and individuals still operated under pressures to conform unthinkingly to religious, national, and political norms. However, it is naive to think that people develop values out of whole cloth, or even reinvent the wheel to develop a personal set of values. Often, becoming freer and developing one's own values meant that the patient took on the therapist's secular values.

Therapists as People with Values

I suggest that we come full circle and focus on therapists as people, not only as puppets in thrall to their own counter-transferential issues but as individuals with sets of beliefs and values. Some of those values will be congruent with those of their patients; some will be in conflict. And values congruency is not always a good thing: a narcissistic therapist and a narcissistic patient can be quite comfortable with each other and reinforce each other's values. However, in my opinion, not much good would be accomplished. (For example, a philandering therapist could see a patient's affairs as growth-producing rather than as evidence of problems with commitment and intimacy.)

I want to speak about some of the values conflicts I have experienced in my own practice as examples of some of the more general issues introduced earlier.

Who am I as the therapist? I am the oldest daughter of four children born to Polish Jews who survived the Holocaust. I grew up in an observant home in a South Jersey rural farming community, where my family was not only one of the few Jews but certainly the only family that kept kosher and kept the Sabbath. I became the interface, the translator of English and America to my parents. Although not always comfortable, I had the privilege of spanning two cultures. I read widely and observed carefully; it was natural that I become an anthropologist or psychologist. Certain that it would be difficult to get kosher meat in Borneo, I elected to do my field work within the therapeutic setting.

I attend an Orthodox synagogue, I am married and have two children, two cats, and one dog. As a licensed psychologist in the state of Georgia, I have been in full time private practice for eighteen years and serve as the director of a private group practice. I am an unabashed feminist and was one of the founding mothers of the Feminist Therapy Collective in Philadelphia (now the Women's Therapy Center). Not all my values line up neatly; some are in conflict and require compromise solutions on my part, or simply learning to live with paradox. Like my patients, I frequently struggle to figure out what is baby and what is bath water. This is the compilation of beliefs, values, and experience I bring to a therapy session.

This Yom Kippur (Day of Atonement) story evokes the conflict between self-actualization and self-transcendence.

During a part of the Yom Kippur service, the rabbi was overcome with the intense emotions of the day and flinging himself on the floor prostrate, cried out, "O Lord, please forgive me. Before you, I am nothing, I am nobody." The cantor, equally overcome with the holiness of the day, also flung himself prostrate on the floor and cried out, "O Lord, please forgive me. Before you, I am nothing, I am nobody." In a little while, one of the less notable congregants was also overwhelmed with the solemnity of the day and threw himself prostrate on the floor, crying out "O Lord, please forgive me. Before you, I am nothing, I am nobody." The cantor caught the rabbi's eye, shrugged, and in a whisper behind his hand said, "Look who thinks he's nobody!"

Lesson: You need to have a self in order to transcend it.

Making a self and transcending a self are basic issues within a marriage, and come to the fore in the process of marital therapy.

Jane and Thomas, both in their late thirties and the parents of two children, had been married for seventeen years when they sought therapy. The presenting issue was that as Thomas became more and more intense about his Judaism, he wanted Jane to observe along with him. Jane experienced this as a coercive dragging into territories she had no desire to explore. Thomas was pained by Jane's lack of support and felt that in this area, as in others with her, he could not please her, that he could just not be good enough. He had been brought up in a traditional Jewish home: although not Sabbath-observant, his family kept kosher, celebrated the holidays, and attended synagogue, and Thomas had been sent to the budding Jewish day school in town rather than the local public school. Thomas was the oldest of four children and was very much the coparent in the family. His life myth was the golden boy who could do no wrong in his family's eyes. After his own children were born and started day school, his interest in Judaism surfaced and his greatest pleasure in life was to learn Torah with a number of local *rebeyim* (plural of rabbi but not in connotation of pulpit rabbi; rather, the scholar who dedicates his life to teaching and learning more Torah). Thomas and his father owned clothing stores that were open on the Sabbath and Thomas in fact went to work after he attended Orthodox Sabbath services.

Jane grew up in a family that identified itself as Jewish but observed very few of the traditions. Her father was a pleasant, passive man who stayed at his hardware store as much as he could and avoided her mother, who could best be described as of the Southern belle/harpy variety. Her mother was a bitter woman who felt she had been betrayed by her husband's inability to earn a *really* good living. Much of her anger spilled out on her oldest daughter, Jane, who even as a child couldn't figure out what she did that was so bad that Mom couldn't love her. Jane's myth was to be the Despised One, the bad one who deserved nothing good and who would never come to a good end.

This couple's battlefield was a white tablecloth for the Sabbath table. Thomas wanted Jane to make Friday night special and festive; he asked her to purchase and place a white tablecloth on the dinner table Friday night. Jane saw this as the first step down a slippery slope leading to full blown orthodoxy and a totally alien way of life. Jane's issue with Thomas was that she wanted a large house for her family, but she felt that Thomas would limit his earning power and never be able to afford more than what they had. Her assessment of her husband fit with her general life story, anyway. She didn't really deserve to have a house, much less a successful husband. It fit that she had a husband who made unrealistic demands on her, just like her mother did. Thomas, who had always been the good child, couldn't understand why he failed to find favor in his wife's eyes.

In an interesting play on the theme of self-actualization and religion, if Thomas were encouraged to follow his passion for Jewish learning and observance, he could very well lose his wife. Thomas felt great embarrassment that he drove to his synagogue because he did not live within walking distance. Any house that he could afford within walking distance to the *shul* (synagogue) would not be an improvement over the one he was currently in. More affordable houses were outside the orthodox community boundaries. For Jane to have her dream house, Thomas would have to give up his dream of being able to walk to *shul* on the Sabbath and on holidays. If Jane could get her house, would she lose her husband?

The couple bickered about the tablecloth for a good while before realizing that for both, the tablecloth was a white flag of surrender. And just like a cigar is sometimes nothing more than a good smoke, a white tablecloth can be just a table covering. When Thomas assured Jane that he loved her and that she was a wonderful wife and mother (which she was but had doubted for many years) and was deserving of love and material goods, she could let him have a white tablecloth.

Jane never felt that the time Thomas spent learning was a problem for her; he could devote himself as much as he wanted to his Jewish passions. His need for her involvement was the issue for her. In reality, it is impossible to have a traditional Jewish home without a wife's involvement. (Our local rabbi says that if a man becomes observant, you have an observant man; if a woman becomes observant, you have an observant family.) When Jane no longer felt Thomas would usurp her control over her own life, she was able to increase the amount of ritual in their home. Thomas struggled with the concept of a new house that he could afford and that Jane would like versus a house within walking distance of the synagogue. At one point, he happened to cross paths with the *rebbetzin* (rabbi's wife) who asked why he looked so unhappy. He explained that he constantly worried over his inability to become totally observant. She replied that if his children saw their father's response to his Judaism as one of constant pain and discouragement, there would be very little in it that they would want for themselves. Her words lightened his heart. He traveled to Israel and Baltimore (a bastion of orthodoxy) frequently, often with and sometimes without his children. He tried to make his observance of Judaism as joyous as possible. He and Jane bought a house in a neighborhood Jane loved. It was not within walking distance; however, Jane understood and appreciated the sacrifice for her and began working full-time (rather than part-time) to help pay for the house and the children's day school and college tuitions.

Were I a totally secular therapist, would I have viewed Thomas' love of Orthodox Judaism as obsessional or deviant? It doesn't make sense in a world of electric labor-saving devices and conveniences that in order to refrain from working one must refrain from driving on the Sabbath. Or would I have told him that if he needed the intensity of observance to feel fulfilled he should "go for it"? In order to empower Jane, would I have supported her need to hold the line vis à vis a white tablecloth? Would this couple have been perceived as so different in their basic needs and values that divorce would have been the only acceptable answer?

Understanding that neither patient, therapist, nor therapeutic technique operates within a values vacuum, E. Mansell Pattison suggests that
the therapist is obligated to: 1) be aware of his or her own values; 2) be
aware of the patient's values; 3) define the patient-therapist-society consensus within which the patient is working and if he or she cannot work
within that consensus with integrity, to refuse to treat, and refer the patient to a therapist who can work within that context; and 4) maintain
respect for the patient's integrity so that the patient is able to develop a
distinction between the values of the therapist and the patient "even
though they may be in agreement." (p.113)

Some examples from my own practice follow Pattison:

In order to help her achieve more in school and follow a more structured
study schedule, a prominent Jewish family had allowed its teen-aged daughter to board at a local school. While there, she was invited to attend charismatic Christian services and was very attracted by the people and the spirit
she felt there. She decided to convert to Christianity but did not tell her family what she had done for a couple of years. When her family learned of her
conversion, they brought in a Jewish deprogrammer to change her commitment. However, this young woman held fast to her ideals and refused to alter
her conversion. When she decided to marry a Christian young man (the
nephew of the minister who had converted her), she wanted her parents to
attend her wedding and, as they had done for their other married children,
provide an elaborate wedding reception for her in the church.

Her parents, who were in therapy with me at the time, asked for help in
deciding what to do. Were I a non-Jewish therapist, I suppose I could have
seen their daughter's choices as part of her separation and individuation and
as instrumental in forming her own sense of identity. Although I saw it less as
an expression of anger and rejection of her parents and more as seduction by
her peer group, as a Jew I felt terribly uncomfortable with the whole situation. I told the family that any direction in helping them make their decisions
would arise from my own set of values (which they shared in large measure).
Because they were parents who had had difficulty setting firm boundaries
with some of their children, we decided that the daughter had done an excellent job of teaching her parents, through her own behavior, to hold firm to
articles of belief. The parents attended the wedding as guests and did not
provide a wedding reception; they did not celebrate joy they did not feel.

A thirty-eight-year-old Jewish mother of two boys came to see me because her five-year-old son had been diagnosed with an inoperable brain tumor a year ago and was now in the last stages of dying. She had been in therapy before and felt that she had greatly benefitted from it. She and her husband had a loving relationship, but there were areas which she could not discuss with him. Although both were Jewish, she was more knowledgeable and committed in practice. As her child's condition had worsened over the year, she had consulted her rabbi for spiritual help. Her rabbi was a very kind, warm man who responded to her request with psychological support. He told her that it was okay to feel anger with G-d over her son's death. Although she indicated to him that she needed something more from him than psychological support (she had already read Kübler Ross and anticipated the stages of mourning), he was unable to give her more religious solace. As she and I talked over the kind of funeral service she wanted for her son, I mentioned to her that the Kaddish (the prayer said during the funeral and at specified, frequent times during the coming years) makes no reference to death. It is a public prayer. Mourners say it in full view of the congregation (the congregation responds in unison as the chorus to the mourner's recitations). The Kaddish is an affirmation of G-d's greatness and glory. It is a prayer of praise and not of mourning. It is understood that after a person has experienced intense pain and loss from the death of a loved one, it is an act of courage and affirmation of belief to stand up in public and to praise G-d. Because it must be said in public, it is also an expression of the mourner's continued tie to the Jewish people. At the time of the most intense isolation and emotional loss, the mourner still belongs and is not alone. Ironically, in this situation, her rabbi gave psychological support and her psychologist offered religious counsel.

Death, grief, and loss and how to make sense of them are frequent concerns within people's lives. Family therapists have often used rituals, most often created by the family and/or the therapist, to encapsulate and symbolize a number of family problems, including those related to death. When appropriate, I have talked about the Jewish ritual of *yartzeit,* the anniversary remembrance of a family member's death marked by the lighting of a twenty-four hour *yartzeit* candle. For example, the father and husband of a family with two college-aged sons had quietly and intensely suffered from severe, debilitating, and medication-resistant depressions over a span of twenty years. Only his wife knew the extent of these depressions. Two weeks before Thanksgiving, he methodically summarized the family's financial affairs and after making sure that his wife was at work, used his car exhaust hose to commit suicide. The family grieved intensively, making use of family and individual therapy as needed. Thanksgiving, taken up with the funeral process, was a blur in time to them. By Christmas, the loss had become more focused. We discussed the *yartzeit* candle as something within my culture and the family decided to purchase a very large red candle. They lit the candle at the start of the holiday and extinguished it at the end with plans to save it from year to year, lighting wick to wick of the new candle when it finally burned out. The imagery of the soul as light made a transition from one frame to another through the *yartzeit* candle ritual.

A grieving young mother had been referred to me because her eight month old child had died from Sudden Infant Death Syndrome (SIDS). She had been referred to me because as a psychologist I often work with issues of death and loss, and because we had also lost a baby to SIDS. During the first session, the mother wept in my office and talked about her grief. She and I were quickly forming a therapeutic alliance. Toward the end of the session, she asked what my ideas of heaven were. She was a committed Christian and it was very important to her that her therapist share her views of the afterlife. I responded by telling her that as a Jew, my belief was limited to a sense of *olam ha bah* (the world to come) but without a great deal of emphasis on the details of an after-life. She thanked me for my time and indicated that she needed a therapist who held the same values that she did. This young woman was not resistant, nor in denial; she intuitively knew that her set of values required a different kind of experience than she would have with me. We parted on friendly terms; I hope that she was able to find a Christian therapist who could enter her frame of belief about life after death.

Ed, a bright, highly successful thirty-three-year-old business man entered therapy torn by a sense of responsibility to his wife and two young children and his desire to leave his family to be with his girlfriend of two years. He described his wife, Susan, as a "plain Jane," pleasant, a little plump, not very pretty, not exciting but a good wife and mother. His girlfriend Wanda was beautiful, smart, sexy, sophisticated, and married to someone else. However, if Ed left Susan, Wanda promised to leave her husband for Ed. When Ed entered therapy, there were many ways in which he felt he and Susan were unsuited: she was not ambitious, open to new experiences, witty, or sharp. She was very much a product of her restricted Southern Baptist upbringing. Although he had come from a similar background, he had been driven to achieve and expand himself. He presented himself as an intelligent, insightful man married to a dull, plodding woman. As his life story unfolded, it was apparent that he was "Dobie Gillis," the sitcom character who ardently and disastrously pursues beautiful women and never gets them. The only girl who wants him is the unattractive "Zelda." Wanda was a winner, the girl he would have wanted as a boy and never would have gotten. Wanda was a trophy, Susan was an albatross. It certainly would have enhanced his image of himself to parade Wanda on his arm.

When Ed examined the "Dobie Gillis" myth of himself, he was able to see how much of his life he had constructed to fit that myth of the boy who has to settle for second best in his love life. It followed that because Susan had chosen him, she was second rate. As therapy progressed and Ed understood himself better, he was able to focus on his relationship with Susan and perceive her differently, and to question the nature of his relationship with Wanda. Rank narcissism would have compelled him to go with the willowy, good-looking Wanda. However, more reflection allowed him to see the myth that had propelled him and to begin to make purposive changes in his own life. He also began to understand that he was a minor player in Wanda's own life drama. Wanda, who wanted children desperately, had married a man with a vasectomy. He had not told her of this until after they were married. Her parents would never approve of divorce and she refused to tell them of his vasectomy. Wanda's central life myth was the Martyr. As Ed terminated with Wanda, she entered therapy with her husband. Since I knew that I personally did not approve of Ed's taking off with Wanda, it was important that Ed come to a decision about this relationship based on his understanding of his life story and not merely to please his therapist. Ed elected to stay with Susan and with his therapy. I mention this to dispel the myth of a Svengali-type of power that therapists have over their patients. Patients who find themselves at odds with their therapists, whether for right or wrong reasons, often vote with their feet: they terminate therapy. Ed was able to claim ownership of his therapy and his own insights.

An important value within therapy itself is the importance of separation and individuation in the development of an autonomous self. Throughout the developmental cycle of the child and certainly for the adolescent and young adult, it is crucial to see oneself as different and separate from the "authority" or the "parent." The child or young person who can not do this remains dependent and handicapped by the inability to make decisions autonomously. In Eric Erikson's eight stages of man, he discusses this as the conflict between intimacy and isolation. The striving for intimacy generates a need to fuse one's identity with someone else's. The need for isolation reflects an unwillingness to blend oneself with others. The healthy person finds a balance between these two needs.

At times, I suspect that we in the field of psychotherapy have focused on separation and individuation, on becoming a separate self, with very little emphasis on being connected and belonging. Perhaps because our focus has been on people who cannot successfully disconnect from families of origin, we have taken separation as an ultimate good. It isn't. Now we work with people who do not know how to commit or attach; we diagnose disorders of intimacy. By encouraging patients to focus only on themselves, we have allowed people to get stuck in the adolescent stage of life. It is important that we promote movement to the next stages: those of generativity (versus stagnation) and ego integrity (versus despair).

> Michael was a thirty-three-year-old married man with a young baby. Although he loved his wife, he feared being emotionally intimate with her. As we discussed this fear, it was clear that Michael, the son of an alcoholic father and a critical mother, had not felt safe in being dependent on anyone. His life lesson had been "you better take care of it yourself because there is no one else to do it for you." In many ways, he has been a "Lone Ranger." In order to survive as a child, he needed actively to fight against feeling trust or dependency on anyone else, particularly a family member. Now married, he feared becoming too emotionally dependent on his wife, sure that she would also abandon him. Because intimacy can lead to dependency, intimacy must be avoided. As we pursued this discussion during our session, Michael experienced the "aha" phenomena and saw this fear of intimacy as something

within his spiritual life as well for he had also stopped himself from feeling intimate with G-d. The motto of self-sufficiency and self-reliance has blocked Michael from his wife and his own spiritual strivings.

John was a forty-year-old-single business man. Following his college graduation, he had sought additional training in international relations and had worked extensively in Southeast Asian refugee camps. Although he had experienced intense personal satisfaction from this work, a number of factors had intervened making it difficult for him to return to it. Although he was successful as a businessman, it was not a fulfilling life for him and he wanted to return to refugee work. John had sought therapy because of ongoing depression, alcoholism, and a propensity for engaging in love relationships that failed within three months. John then mourned the relationship's demise for a very long time, often longer than the relationship itself had lasted. John's mother, whom he had adored as a child, had died from cancer when he was fourteen. It took him a while to remember how old he had been at the time of her death and the circumstances surrounding it. He had not attended her funeral nor had he visited her grave. His father was an alcoholic, a highly successful tax attorney, and a bitter and critical father. In seeking relationships that quickly ended in the death of the relationship, John was giving himself the opportunity to mourn his loss, without fully realizing the loss he mourned was that of his mother. When he realized that the continuation of his life story was being blocked by his unfulfilled need to grieve, he was able to go back to his mother's grave and make his peace with her in a private funeral ceremony. He still struggles with alcohol consumption but has been able to drink far less. I suppose we could look at his desire to work in refugee camps as a co-dependent expression of the desire to fix everyone else's problems rather than his own. However, he and I have chosen to look at this altruistic desire as a positive good in his life, as a serious choice for a meaningful life. It is not a running-away-from (as some of his other choices have been), but a positive going-toward.

As therapists, we need to recognize that we live within a set of values and meanings. As we choose that set for ourselves, like the pregnant mother who eats not only for herself but also for her developing fetus, we are also choosing that set for our patients. That values-set defines for us the "normal" or mental health, and selects the goals for psychotherapy. I as an individual carry a set of values, and like truth-in-labelling, hang the following words on my wall:

> If I am not for myself, who will be for me? And if I am only for myself, what am I? And if not now, when? (Hillel, Pirke Avos I:14)

SELECT BIBLIOGRAPHY

Books

Baumeister, Roy F. *Meanings of Life*. New York: Guilford Press, 1991.

Berne, Eric. *Games People Play*. New York: Ballantine Books, 1964.

Erikson, Eric. *Childhood and Society*. New York: Norton, 1950.

Feinstein, Moshe, in Hershler, M. (Ed.) *Sefer Halacha Urefua,* Halacha and Medicine. Jerusalem/Chicago: Regensberg Institute, 1980.

Frankl, Victor E. *The Unheard Cry for Meaning: Psychotherapy and Humanism*. New York: Simon & Schuster, 1978.

Fromm-Reichman, Freida. *Principles of Intensive Psychotherapy*. Chicago: University of Chicago Press, 1950.

Kushner, Harold. *When All You've Ever Wanted Isn't Enough: the Search for a Life that Matters*. New York: Simon & Schuster, Inc., 1987.

Lasch, Christopher. *The Culture of Narcissism: American Life in an Age of Diminishing Expectations*. New York: Norton, 1978.

Lovinger, Robert J. *Working with Religious Issues in Therapy*. New York: Jason Aronson, Inc., 1984.

May, Rollo. *The Cry for Myth*. New York: W.W. Norton & Company, Inc., 1991.

Pattison, E. Mansell. "Morality, Guilt, and Forgiveness in Psychotherapy" In E.M. Pattison, Ed. *Clinical Psychiatry and Religion*. Boston: Little, Brown, and Company, 1969.

Peck, M. Scott. *The Road Less Traveled: A New Psychology of Love, Traditional Values, and Spiritual Growth*. New York: Simon & Schuster, Inc. 1978.

Perls, Frederick S. *In and Out of the Garbage Pail*. Lafayette, Calif.: Real People Press, 1969.

Rogers, Carl R. *Client-Centered Therapy.* Boston: Houghton Mifflin, 1951.

Roman, P. M. and Trice, H. M. (Eds.) *The Sociobiology of Psychotherapy.* New York: Jason Aronson, 1974.

Seligman, Martin E. P. *Helplessness: On Depression, Development and Death.* San Francisco: Freeman, 1975.

Szasz, Thomas S. *The Ethics of Psychoanalysis.* New York: Dell, 1965.

Wallach, M. A. and Wallach, L. *Psychology's Sanction for Selfishness: The Error of Egoism in Theory and Therapy.* San Francisco: Freeman, 1983.

Articles

Buie, James. "'Me' Decades Generate Depression." *Monitor* 19, no. 10. Washington, DC: American Psychological Association, (1988).

Hankoff, L. D. "The Role of Values in Psychotherapy: Sources and Conflicts." In C. S. Naiman, Ed. *Proceedings of the Associations of Orthodox Jewish Scientists,* (1984): 7:11–34.

Ragan, C., H. N. Malony, B. Beit-Hallahmi. "Psychologists and Religion: Professional Factors and Personal Belief," *Review of Religious Research,* (1980): 21:208–17.

Samler, J. "Changes in Values: a Goal in Counseling," *Journal of Counseling Psychology,* (1960): 7:32–9.

Creation, Cosmology, and Ethics

Nancey Murphy

When I look at your heavens, the work of your fingers,
the moon and the stars that you have established;
What are human beings that you are mindful of them,
mortals that you care for them? (Psalm 8:3–4)

Introduction

A common view of science, ethics, and religion in recent decades has been that science is value-free and religion is nothing but values. By these lights the paper that follows is highly unorthodox. I shall claim, first, that theology gives us genuine *knowledge* about ourselves, our cosmos, and its relation to God; that science and theology, therefore, have a lot to say to one another; and that a positive relation between science and theology has consequences for both scientific practice and larger ethical issues.

This paper has grown out of work for two conferences. The first, sponsored by the Vatican Observatory, was a conference on the implications of contemporary scientific cosmology for our understanding of God's action in the world. I was reflecting on the work afterward with a cosmologist from South Africa who is deeply involved in peace and justice issues there, and asking what difference our abstruse reasoning about the origins of the universe made for people who were suffering and dying.

Shortly thereafter I was invited to a conference sponsored by The Association for Religion and Intellectual Life, whose purpose was to consider the place of faith in higher education and the efficacy of faith-informed learning for meeting the world's needs. As a philosopher and theologian involved in the dialogue between theology and the natural sciences, I was forced again to ask: how does this all matter for life-and-death issues? This paper is an attempt to address that question. I shall actually take up four interrelated questions:

1. What does my own Christian faith have to do with my academic work?
2. What are the possibilities for a positive relation between theology and science?
3. What implications would such a relation have for scientific practice?
4. What implications might such a relation have for life-and-death issues?

My Faith and Work

A bit of autobiography is perhaps not inappropriate in a volume on narrative ethics. I teach at Fuller Theological Seminary. Fuller's identity comes not from a denominational affiliation; rather, it identifies itself as Evangelical. It's not clear exactly what that means. In the first instance, it surely has to do with trying to serve churches and future church leaders who identify themselves with the Evangelical movement in the United States and elsewhere. On this account, Fuller is an odd place for me. I've never belonged to a self-proclaimed Evangelical church. My roots are Catholic, but I'm currently a member of the Church of the Brethren—a church I've joined because of its Anabaptist (radical reformation) heritage and, in particular, its pacifist tradition.

So why am I teaching at a Calvinistic place like Fuller? Well, another way to answer the question about Evangelical identity is by situating

Evangelicals on a theological spectrum somewhere between Fundamentalists and Liberals. This is where I find myself. I see the Fundamentalists as having not yet taken seriously the past two hundred years of intellectual history. But I can't identify with the Liberals either.

Liberal theology follows a pattern set at the end of the eighteenth century by Immanuel Kant in making a sharp distinction between the realms of faith (religion) and knowledge (science). For Kant, religion belonged in the category of ethics. For Friedrich Schleiermacher (1768–1834), the 'father' of modern theology, there were three realms: the realm of knowledge, the realm of morality, and the realm of religion, having to do with a special sort of awareness or feeling. And so, for example, the doctrine of creation does not give us information about the beginning of the universe; rather, it leaves all questions of origins to science and speaks instead of our sense of the absolute dependence of all things on God. Today's heirs of this tradition generally make some sort of distinction between the realm of facts, knowledge, science, and the realm of values, meaning, faith.

I did my theological studies in a liberal setting, the Graduate Theological Union in Berkeley, but I wasn't converted. The trouble was that I arrived there with an a priori idea of what theology must be. I had just come from the philosophy department at the University of California at Berkeley, where I felt like the last Christian on earth. I had been studying philosophy of science there, and in answer to the questions that inevitably arose about the rationality of Christian belief, I had come to suppose that Christian doctrines functioned similarly to scientific theories—they were explanations of experience. Only here the experience was not from the laboratory but from living the Christian life.

Much of my time since then has been spent developing this theory in suitable academic detail. My conclusion: When done properly, theological theories constitute *knowledge* in exactly the same sense as do the theories of science.

Notice that I've switched categories, from talking about religion and faith to talking about theology. I do not want to try to draw close parallels between *religion* and science. But if we take *theology* to be the systematic exposition of the beliefs of a religious community, in such a way as to show their logical relations to one another and the sort of rational support that can be given for them, then we have an academic discipline that does bear some striking similarities to science.[1] The facts of Christian experience, if properly evaluated and interpreted, provide information about the character and work of God in the world. In this sense, theology is not merely human reflection on ultimate values; it is genuine knowledge about the way things are, about ultimate *Reality*.

How Should Theology and Science Relate?

There are three standard positions on the question of what science and religion (or theology) have to do with one another.

1. The conflict model expresses the views of the creationists: science and Christianity are competing for the same turf.

2. The so-called two-worlds model is the view commonly found among heirs of Kant and Schleiermacher: science and religion are such different enterprises that they cannot possibly conflict or even affect one another. Often proponents of this view go on to emphasize the complementarity of science and faith. Science gives us the facts; religion gives us the "meanings" for human existence. Science gives us technology; religion gives us ethical guidance for its use.

3. The third position, the interactive model, is a minority view but is gaining in acceptance. This is the view I favor. Because I believe that theology gives us genuine knowledge about God, human beings, and the future, what theology has to say sometimes connects (positively or negatively) with what the sciences have to say. A complete view of reality requires that we take both science and theology into account, and we must strive for consistency if we find conflicts.[2]

In this view the Bible does not replace science (as it does for creationists). Nor does it complement it on some other plane; rather, it complements (completes) it in a very straightforward sense. This means that theology learns from science and also—a much more startling claim, I'm sure—science can occasionally learn from theology. I'll come back to this latter issue in considering the implications for scientific practice.

An Example

Let me illustrate my proposal regarding the interaction between science and theology with an example from scientific cosmology. This issue is what cosmologists call the fine-tuning of the universe. The current state of the universe can best be explained by assuming an initial event, called the Big Bang, between ten and twenty billion years ago. In the earliest stages, the 'stuff' of the universe was not yet differentiated into matter and energy. Later, atoms of the lightest gasses formed. Stars congealed from clouds of gas between one and five billion years into the universe's history. The heat and pressure inside stars allowed for the "cooking" of the heavier elements, such as carbon. At a certain stage in the development the stars exploded, and by this means the heavier elements were distributed throughout the universe, providing the material for planets and ultimately for living beings.

Calculations show that a number of factors at the beginning of the universe had to be adjusted in a remarkably precise way for the process to result in a habitable universe. One factor is the mass of the universe; others include the four basic forces—gravitation, electromagnetism, and the strong and weak nuclear forces—and the ratios of the masses and charges of various subatomic particles. Calculations show that if any of these numbers had been much different than it is the universe would not have turned out to be a place in which intelligent life of any sort could exist. Life requires a universe with a sufficient time span. It requires the existence of elements heavier than the gasses that constituted it in the beginning. It requires stars and planets. In countless ways things could have gone wrong, leaving the universe an uninhabited waste.

Let me give a few examples of the fine-tuning that was required. The density of matter in the universe is a critical factor. If the mass were much greater, gravitational attraction would too easily overcome the expansive force resulting from the initial explosion and the universe would recollapse before stars, planets, and life had a chance to form. (And, of course, if the gravitational force were stronger, the same result could be expected.) On the other hand, if the mass were much smaller, then the universe would spread out and cool off too quickly for life to develop.

Carbon is one of the basic elements needed for life, and many of the calculations have to do with necessary conditions for its formation and distribution. If the nuclear strong force were 1 percent weaker or stronger, carbon would not form within the stellar ovens. In fact, it has been calculated that the strong force had to be within .8 and 1.2 times its actual strength for there to be any elements at all with atomic weights greater than 4. Finally, if electromagnetism had been stronger, stars would not explode and the heavier elements needed for life would not be available.

The nuclear weak force's very weakness makes our sun burn gently for billions of years instead of blowing up like a bomb. Had this force been appreciably stronger, stars of this sort would be impossible. But if it were much weaker the universe would be composed entirely of helium.

Here are some remarkable numbers: The ratio of the strength of electromagnetism to the strength of gravity appears to be crucial. Changes in either force by 1 part in 10 to the 40th power (10 followed by 40 zeros) would spell catastrophe for stars like our sun.

Electrons and protons have equal but opposite charges. It has been estimated that a charge difference of more than 1 part in 10 billion would mean that there could be no macroscopic objects; that is, there could be no solid bodies weighing more than about a gram.

The ratio between gravity and the nuclear weak force may have to be adjusted as accurately as 1 part in 10 to the 100th power to avoid either a swift collapse of the universe or an explosion.

Cosmologists began noting these strange coincidences in the 1950s; by now several books have appeared with page after page of such conclusions.[3] What are we to make of these results? Some scientists have been led to ask if there must not be a God after all. Others have proposed different explanations. One response is to say that it *is* very remarkable that, from among all the possible universes, the one that exists happens to be suitable for life, but this is simply a matter of chance.

Another explanation is that there are a vast number of universes, either preceding and following this one or contemporaneous with it but beyond the range of our observation. All have different basic numbers. By random variation, then, one can expect one or more universes to have values suited for life, and of course only such a universe would contain observers to wonder at its being so. And there are other, more exotic explanations as well.

However, the chance hypothesis is really not an explanation; it is better understood as a claim that there can be no explanation. The assorted many-universes hypotheses are as yet unconfirmed scientifically and may not in fact be scientific at all. It is not unreasonable, then, to suggest that science has reached the very edge of its competence. There may *never* be a scientific answer to the puzzling question of why the universe turned out, against such tremendous odds, to be life-supporting.

I suggest that we have reached a point here where science and theology intersect, for if the Jewish or Christian or Islamic doctrine of creation is true, it follows naturally enough from the premise that God intended a universe with intelligent life that the physical prerequisites for life would be provided. While the scientific evidence does not demand a theological answer, one has to admit that the doctrine of creation provides a neat answer to the cosmologists' puzzle.

So this is an instance of complementarity. Science reaches the boundary of its explanatory power; theology picks up the task at that point. I have made a stronger claim, though, about the relations between theology and science: I have claimed that genuine interaction is possible. Let us look, now, at how the two disciplines can affect one another through this point of intersection.

Implications for Theology

I have argued elsewhere that the fine-tuning of the universe opens up possibilities for a new design argument, but one vastly different from those of the eighteenth century. Earlier natural theologians supposed that they could construct arguments that would stand on their own, apart from the tradition and related historical and experiential factors that lent them credibility. I claim instead that fine-tuning merely provides *additional* evidence for a hypothesis (the existence of a Creator) that is already supported in other, more traditional ways.[4]

A second, perhaps more important influence to be expected from cosmology is a deeper insight into the purposes of God and into God's relationship with us. The psalmist writes:

> When I look at your heavens, the work of your fingers,
>   the moon and the stars that you have established;
> What are human beings that you are mindful of them,
>   mortals that you care for them? (Psalm 8:3–4)

How much more than the psalmist are we able to appreciate the wonder of the cosmos itself and, with these recent discoveries, to appreciate the fact that, in a certain sense, it all appears to have been created with us in mind.

Since the Copernican revolution humans have been removed from the center of the universe. We've also discovered how small our planet is compared to the vastness of the universe, and how short our history is compared to its age. Our view of the natural world has been 'de-anthropocentrized.' However, the present cosmological results show that in order for God to have creatures such as ourselves, the whole universe had to be created pretty much as it is. It had to have about as much matter as it does—as many stars, galaxies, planets—and it had to be about as old as it is. We are *not* at the center of the universe, but for believers it is certainly possible to see ourselves as the point or end of it all. We can say, literally, that all the stars in the heavens, even the billions we cannot see, were created for our sake.

Let me stress again: I am not arguing that we could draw these anthropocentric conclusions from cosmology alone. Rather, I am saying that those of us whose views of the place of humankind in God's universe are shaped by the biblical creation stories find our theological perspective confirmed in a rather striking manner by the cosmologists' results. (Showing that the biblical worldview has evidence of its own is beyond the scope of this paper.)

In speaking of a biblical view of humankind's place in the cosmos, however, I need to be specific about my interpretation of the *point* of the creation stories (Gen. 1:1–2:4a and Gen. 2:4b–24). I am assuming (with the majority of contemporary scholars) that the point of the stories is not to provide a chronology of events (as creationists assume), but rather to speak of the character of the created order and of God's relation to it: of God's sovereignty and freedom with respect to the cosmos; of the goodness and order of the cosmos. Most important for our purposes is the position humans are assigned in these stories. In the Yahwist's account (Gen. 2:4bff.) the special relation of the earth creature (*'adam*) to God is symbolized in its animation by the divine breath and its dominion over the animals. In the Priestly account (Gen. 1:1ff.) the creation of humans is the climax of the creative drama, and their special relation to God is expressed in the divine decision to make them "in our image, after our likeness."

So human beings (alone) were created to have fellowship with God; they alone can articulate their praise of God; they alone can both hear God's word and see God's designs in the rest of creation.

In light of these stories, it makes sense to look at the results from cosmology and say—not how odd, how surprising that the universe happened to be suited for intelligent life—but rather, how wonderfully it suits God's purposes.

Implications for Scientific Practice

My third question is: What are the implications for scientific practice of the kind of relation between science and theology that I am affirming? Here I want to draw on a book by Nicholas Wolterstorff on the relations between science and religion, which I believe has received too little attention. In *Reason Within the Bounds of Religion,* Wolterstorff points out (drawing on the best of recent philosophy of science) that scientific theories are never determined solely by the facts. The inevitable logical gap between theory and data indicates that the weighing of theories must always involve other considerations besides the data. Using historical examples, he shows that one of these other considerations is scientists' beliefs as to what constitutes an acceptable *sort* of theory on the matter under consideration.

> We can call these *control* beliefs. They include beliefs about the requisite logical or aesthetic structure of a theory, beliefs about the entities to whose existence a theory may correctly commit us, and the like. Control beliefs function in two ways. Because we hold them we are led to *reject* certain sorts of theories—some because they are inconsistent with those beliefs; others because, though consistent with our control beliefs, they do not comport well with those beliefs. On the other hand control beliefs also lead us to *devise* theories. We want theories that are consistent with our control beliefs.[5]

Wolterstorff notes that control beliefs can be derived from either theological or philosophical positions. His examples show that some have had a positive effect in science while others have inhibited its progress. For example, Descartes allowed his philosophical control belief that there can be no action at a distance to prevent him from accepting the theory of gravitation. Ernst Mach held a philosophical control belief prohibiting theories postulating non-sensory entities, which led him to reject many theories of his day but also to begin to reconstruct physics on a new basis.

Both of these examples are of the effect of philosophical control beliefs on the progress of science. However, Wolterstorff argues that if we are convinced of the truth of Christianity, then it is appropriate for convictions judged to be essential to that belief system to play, insofar as possible, the role of control beliefs in scientific and other kinds of theorizing. This is not to say that religious convictions replace stringent scientific testing of theories. Rather, they add additional criteria for choosing which theories to pursue or reject within the range of those that are scientifically acceptable.

Here is an example of this sort of reasoning, again from cosmology. G. F. R. Ellis takes God's omniscience and concern for and attention to each individual in the universe to be central Christian beliefs. These in turn rule out certain models of the universe; namely, those that are infinite in expanse and therefore contain an infinite number of individuals.

While we can (perhaps with some difficulty) envisage the Creator attending to each particle and each individual in the visible part of the universe, if we accept the standard universe models with flat or negative spatial curvature, there are not a finite number of particles but an infinite number; and almost certainly, also an infinite number of individuals. . . . It seems to me to stretch credulity too far that the Creator could succeed in giving the desired attention to an infinite number of beings. . . . The point here is that a mind cannot really have a satisfactory grasp of items of information unless it integrates them one with another, keeping track of the relationship between each one item and all the others through some kind of indexing scheme, but when you have an infinity of items the problem explodes into logical nonsense: you get infinities of infinities of infinities. These disastrous infinities threaten to enter if God has to keep track not only of the items of knowledge, but also of his knowledge of the items of knowledge, and then of these relations also; which I would take as essential for an overall synthesis of the kind presented here to have meaning.

Thus I would suggest that to make the overall view coherent, we must assume *there is a finite number of particles, and of beings, in the universe.*[6]

At present there is no scientific way to arbitrate among the competing models of the universe, and so it remains to be seen whether Ellis's theological-cosmological conclusion will be borne out by future scientific development. If it is, it will be an interesting case of a theological control belief contributing to the progress of science.

Implications of a Combined View for the World's Problems

As mentioned above, the modern dogma has been that science is value-free, and that religion is a matter of personal preference (values). Ethics has been under continual threat of being relegated to the realm of private taste as well. Certainly, insofar as ethical precepts are taken to follow from a religious outlook, they too become a matter of personal preference.

This is in sharp contrast to earlier ages when ethical prescriptions were seen to be rooted in the very nature of reality—as much the case

for ancient Greece as for the Jewish and Christian traditions. For example, Aristotle taught that all things were composed of matter and form.
Form provided a built-in purpose. The good is to act in accordance with
this intrinsic nature; evil is to act against the nature of things.

Much of ancient Israel's morality was based not on the nature of
the cosmos, but on the nature of God and on what God had done in
history. Why rest on the Sabbath? Because God had rested on the sev-
enth day. Why welcome the stranger? Because the Israelites had been
strangers in Egypt.

Similarly, for Christians, the answer to questions about how they
should live were based ultimately on the character of God. Why are
Christians to love their enemies? Because God makes the rain fall on the
just and unjust alike. In the middle ages Christians combined the Greek
philosophical tradition with their own scriptural tradition, and based
ethical demands (natural law) on the will of God as expressed in the created order.

Stephen Toulmin's recent book, *Cosmopolis,*[7] sets out a revisionist account of the transition from medieval and renaissance thought to modern,
and looks ahead at possibilities for a new postmodern worldview. The title of the book refers to a worldview in which social structures (the *polis*)
are seen to mirror the structure or character of the cosmic order, and are
thereby justified as being in accordance with the nature of things. Toulmin offers a persuasive explanation of the prevalent features of modern
thought as a reaction to the loss of cosmopolis. For example, he reads John
Donne's *An Anatomy of the World* as a lament for the loss of cosmopolis:

> 'Tis all in pieces, all Cohaerance gone,
> All just supply, and all Relation.

This is a lament not only for the fragmentation of Europe and of traditional society, but also for the loss of a coherent scientific order. These
various kinds of incoherence—even disrupted weather patterns in England—were all of a piece: the cosmo-political order was coming apart.

I shall borrow Toulmin's analysis to describe our present situation, as
well, as the loss of cosmopolis. Knowledge of the physical world has been

severed from knowledge of its ultimate origin and purpose (religious knowledge), and as a result we have no common point of reference—no grounding in reality—for ethics and politics.

What impact would a view combining theological and scientific insights have on the world's problems? In order not to speak in vague generalities, let me return to the example from cosmology discussed above, and ask what sort of consequences follow from it if we interpret it against the background of the biblical stories of God's creation and redemption.

Environmental Ethics

Christians for many years have thought of the natural world as a stage for human life and history. As such it was seen to have little intrinsic value to God. There was no strong theological tendency to counter those who took biblical language about dominion (see Ps. 8:5–8) as license to exploit and destroy the environment.

The cosmology we have just examined, however, highlights the interconnectedness of human life with its natural environment. We are the result of an unimaginably complex, finely-tuned, fifteen-billion-year process. A better analogy (than that of actors on a stage) to represent our relation to the natural world is to think of ourselves as fruit on a tree. Without the tree, without a healthy tree, we could not be here. Carl Sagan, for all his limitations as a theologian, makes the point nicely in saying that we are made of star dust. Immersion in the world of science, especially contemporary cosmology and astronomy, produces a sense of reverence for the natural world that may be a more effective deterrent to exploitation than any prudential calculations of dire future consequences.

But there is a second motive for environmental consciousness built into a theistic interpretation of contemporary cosmology. Let us think what the process of creation tells us about the character of the Creator.

First, the immense time span speaks of the Creator's patience. True, a thousand years is as a day for God, but we still have to recognize a vast difference between the instantaneous creation that Christians assumed for many years and the slow, painstaking process that current cosmology suggests.

The point I wish to emphasize here is the great respect God seems to show for the integrity of the entities and processes that have been created. Diogenes Allen emphasizes that creation involves God's self-limitation— a withholding of divine power so that other things, things genuinely distinct from God, can exist.

> When God creates, it means that he allows something to exist which is not himself. This requires an act of profound renunciation. He chooses out of love to permit something else to exist, something created to be itself and to exist by virtue of its own interest and value. God renounces his status as to only existent—he pulls himself back, so to speak, in order to give his creation room to exist for its own sake.[8]

This voluntary restraint, exercised for the sake of people *and things* out of respect for their reality, is grace. "The very creation of the world is an act of such grace" (p. 36).

The view that God withholds power to allow for free human actions is commonplace. It has long been recognized that God wants no coerced responses to divine initiatives. But (following Allen) I suggest that we must extend this view of divine self-limitation; speaking not only of free *will* but of free *processes,* going right back to the very beginning of creation. God brings the universe into being with its in-built laws, initial conditions, and potentialities, and allows the entities and processes as they unfold to become "created co-creators."[9] God values and respects the integrity of each new order of being as it emerges. This understanding of God has obvious implications for our attitudes toward the natural world, including a corresponding respect for nature, with its intricate patterns and balances.

The Ethics of Nonresistant Love

Green is 'in' right now, and so I expect that few will have objections to the foregoing conclusions about the environment. Such an argument may be an instance of what a Russian phrase colorfully describes as "beating one's way through an open door." I expect fewer open doors as I address this next issue.

I mentioned before that I joined the Church of the Brethren because of its Anabaptist tradition of nonviolence. The sixteenth-century Anabaptists separated from their Catholic, Calvinist, and Lutheran traditions over the issue of coercion: the church, they believed, was not to employ state force (civil penalties, torture, execution) to coerce religious conformity. A free and informed response was the only response that mattered. The objection to violent coercion in this area was widely generalized to a refusal to participate in armed conflict and in government jobs that inflicted capital punishment.

The Anabaptists and their followers have claimed that the justification for their position lies clearly in the teaching and example of Jesus—paradigmatically in the Sermon on the Mount and later, on another mount, in the crucifixion. If this is so plain a teaching, though, why are Christian pacifists so small a minority? One explanation is offered by John Yoder.

> Most theologies distinguish in some deep way between creation and redemption. For example, according to Martin Luther in classical Protestantism, or . . . H. Richard Niebuhr in recent times, creation and redemption have two different sets of ethical implications. If you derive your value system from creation, you will, for instance, defend the state, which is an institution of creation. If you derive your guidance from redemption alone, then the teachings and example of Jesus can be normative for you, which may lead to nonresistance. But you only have the right to draw nonresistant conclusions from the teachings and example of Jesus if you admit that the realm of creation is governed by other laws and other authorities.[10]

The context of this remark is a commentary on the Prologue of John's Gospel. The point John is making, according to Yoder, is that what is known in Jesus is precisely the same in authority and in meaning as what underlies creation. God has not revealed a different purpose or character through creation than what we now encounter through Jesus.

What I suggest to you is that God's high regard for the freedom and integrity of creatures goes all the way back to the beginning of time; is manifested consistently with the emergence of each new order of being;

and reaches full clarity in the noncoercive, freedom-enhancing practices of Jesus. Seeing this as the *unwavering* will of God, we too must practice the patience of God. And we must take the risks involved in allowing others their freedom; we must be willing to suffer the same fate as Jesus. But we can do it with the hope and expectation that God's good plans for creation—the potential built in from the beginning—will bear fruit in due season.

Let me sum up the argument of this section. God's respect for free processes in the natural world is the overall pattern of divine action, of which God's noncoercive love of human beings is but one instance. Our imitation of the character of God entails both respect for the natural environment and noncoercive love of our enemies.

The Christian church is a justifiable social order only if it is based in the very nature of Reality. Nonviolent resistance to evil is foolish unless Suffering Love is the power behind and before and above all other powers. Christian faith teaches that it is and, I suggest, a discerning eye can see hints of this truth in the fifteen-billion-year history of the cosmos itself.

CONCLUSIONS

Science will be interpreted against the background of some narrative, whether it be biblical creation stories, or Carl Sagan's Evolutionary Naturalism, or even the Enlightenment's autobiography detailing its escape from all traditional narratives. While it has not been possible to give a rationale here for choosing one of these storylines over the others, I do hope to have given a few glimpses of the light shed by the creation narrative on a bit of current scientific work. We have seen, too, some of the ethical implications of the cosmologists' fine-tuning when viewed from the perspective of God's creative purposes.

In addition, I have suggested that it is not out of order for Jewish and Christian scientists to use their own master stories as a source of insights about proper theory formation. We have no guarantee that such choices will always work out for the best, since our ability to discern the scientific consequences of religious commitments is limited; but when they do, the result is a sort of intellectual integrity that has, sadly, often been lacking in the modern era.

NOTES

1. My most thorough account is in *Theology in the Age of Scientific Reasoning* (Ithaca and London: Cornell University Press, 1990).

2. For a sample of (very different) positions that fall into this category, see A. R. Peacocke, *Theology for a Scientific Age* (Oxford: Basil Blackwell, 1990); R. J. Russell, "Finite Creation without a Beginning: The Doctrine of Creation in Relation to Big Bang and Quantum Cosmologies," in Russell, N. Murphy, and C. J. Isham, eds., *Quantum Cosmology and the Laws of Nature: Scientific Perspectives on Divine Action* (Vatican City State: Vatican Observatory, 1993); and N. Wolterstorff, *Reason Within the Bounds of Religion* (Grand Rapids, MI: Eerdmans, 1976).

3. Two prominent books are J. Barrow and F. Tipler, *The Anthropic Cosmological Principle* (Oxford: Oxford University Press, 1986); and John Leslie, *Universes* (London and New York: Routledge, 1989). The figures above are from Leslie.

4. See my "Evidence of Design in the Fine-Tuning of the Universe," in *Quantum Cosmology and the Laws of Nature*.

5. N. Wolterstorff, *Reason Within the Bounds of Religion*, 63–64.

6. G. F. R. Ellis, "The Theology of the Anthropic Principle," in *Quantum Cosmology and the Laws of Nature*.

7. Stephen Toulmin, *Cosmopolis* (New York: Free Press, 1990).

8. Diogenes Allen, *The Traces of God in a Frequently Hostile World* (Cambridge, MA: Cowley, 1981), 35. Allen is much influenced here by the writings of Simone Weil.

9. This is Philip Hefner's term.

10. John Yoder, *He Came Preaching Peace* (Scottdale, PA: Herald Press, 1985), 82.

After Teaching: Wisdom

Theophus (Thee) H. Smith

I did a terrible thing today. I taught a class.
—A college professor, chagrined by a lapse
from his community's norm of liberal learning[1]

I

Teaching a class can rightly be called a "terrible thing," of course, only where some other educational goal is preferred. The following essay enjoins the task of retrieving such a goal from the demise to which it is increasingly liable in our information age, in which education is debased to the transmission of facts, or theories about facts, or even theories about theories. Among the alternatives are various models for teaching as inducement (compare Latin: *e-ducare,* to lead out), as a way of leading, guiding, encouraging, and prodding students toward effecting their own understanding, rather than simply transmitting to them the understandings of others.[2] My point of departure in retrieving such alternatives is a familiar ideal of education in Western societies: to combine the two distinct objectives of (1) liberal learning that fosters critical thinking and conveys a people's cultural heritage, and (2) specialized learning and technical thinking intended primarily for prospective employment. I delineate the two objectives because they tend to diverge in practice,

however compatible they seem in theory (for reasons suggested below).
Moreover, while it may appear that I prefer the former objective, I hope
it will be clear that my real trajectory extends beyond that preference.
(That is to say, the objective of liberal learning also, or in particular,
serves only as my point of departure.) For I do not consider that the goal
of critical thinking and cultural transmission is sufficient in and of itself
to achieve the end that it espouses. In short, I do not consider that goal to
be an independent *telos* of education. My reasons for that judgment, in
fact, provide the main argument and the organizing principle for the
contents of this chapter.

Preparing students for roles of leadership and critical thinking in Western, democratic societies requires their willing or cooperative induction
into a larger vision of society than one provided by their own backgrounds. Those backgrounds are necessarily shaped by individual experiences, as well as the conditions of family, class, and religious or cultural
history. The need to transcend such conditions constitutes the principal
rationale for liberal education: education that "makes free" by liberating
learners *from* both their congenital ignorance and their acquired prejudices, while liberating them *for* intelligent, responsible, and productive
engagements with their fellow citizens and co-workers. A concise statement of this rationale of liberal learning is offered in this opening paragraph of one college bulletin:

> Liberal education should seek to develop free and rational men and women
> committed to the pursuit of knowledge in its fundamental unity, intelli-
> gently appreciative of their common cultural heritage, and conscious of their
> social and moral obligations. Such men and women are best equipped to mas-
> ter the specific skills of any calling and to become mature, competent and
> responsible citizens of a free society.[3]

But such a view of education exceeds the capability of liberal democratic societies to extend beyond a limited, elite minority of learners. For,
as we have discovered through the rigors of historical experience since
the European Enlightenment, liberal cultures programmatically subvert
their own efforts to establish communities committed to their ideals.

Such liberal values as individual autonomy, progress (even at the expense of tradition), and the superiority of rational-literate expression over the alternative rationalities of folk and oral cultures continually frustrate the possibility that diverse individuals and groups will find common ground within a larger, heterogenous nation-state. To the degree, therefore, that social cohesion, reciprocity, and solidarity are prerequisite to the fulfillment of democratic ideals, to that degree our contemporary societies undermine those ideals.

In addition, the conditions for fostering moral persons and communities are also undermined, as ethicist Stanley Hauerwas asserts: "The ethical theory correlative of such societies, namely, the attempt to limit ethics to the obligations incumbent on each other as self-interested units which rationally calculate how best to secure their own survival, is a formula for the disintegration of the moral self."[4] Ethics as individual, rationalized decision-making disintegrates the moral self because it narrows the contexts within which moral selves are social beings, not individuals acting in isolation. An alternative approach, more conducive to the ends espoused, would enlist citizens (and students as prospective citizens) in a larger social vision in a manner that is intrinsically more inclusive than the rational articulation of individual self-interest allows.

In this chapter I combine, as essential elements in the reconstruction of such a social vision, two domains of human experience that have been jettisoned by Enlightenment prescriptions for social progress: the narrative formation of individuals and communities on the one hand, and their religious formation on the other. However, I retrieve these elements with reference to a new issue under discussion in the academy and in society: pluralism. Increased awareness of cultural pluralism provides a substantially new context for articulating the merits of liberal learning over against mere vocational preparation. The fact and features of pluralism distinguish our current context, with its heightened consciousness of difference and diversity. The perspective offered here is not another apologia for the preferences of liberal learning, but is an emendation of those preferences in contemporary terms.

This emendation bears the impress of my own biography as well. A pluralist experience of society and culture is inevitable for African

American scholars like myself, whose ethnic backgrounds often differ sharply from the academic culture of our educational institutions and professional life. Bicultural experience prepares us for multicultural rather than monocultural views of education, society, and the prospects for cultural transformation. In my case, I have reclaimed the black studies curricula of my ethnic background after an undergraduate, liberal studies immersion in the classic texts of Western civilization (the "great books" curriculum of St. John's College, Annapolis, Maryland). In the effort to achieve and maintain personal integration and psychic wholeness, I have had to discover how to bridge those sometimes disparate worlds. As strategies for survival, therefore, I have learned ways to correlate the "culture texts" of my Afro-American experience with those of my Euro-American experience.[5] These experiential correlations led me to the practice of academic and curricular correlations as well, between ethnic studies classics and conventional Western classics. (I return to such correlations in discussing curricula matters below.)

Contemporary discussions of the goals of liberal education converge on one of the most intractable debates in American educational reform today: whether schools and departments should interpolate multicultural studies within conventional curricula, and within programs of instruction based on Western classical texts and disciplinary approaches. I embrace this convergence, yet I am not concerned to argue the cause of multiculturalism on its own terms, for I believe the debate is genuinely intractable. That is to say, the issue invariably creates polarized positions for which no resolution is possible. As philosopher Alasdair MacIntyre claims in *After Virtue,* the contemporary period does not provide us with compatible or coherent criteria for judging such debates.[6] But where adjudication is not possible at the level of theory and analysis, a *modus vivendi* may nonetheless be achieved at the level of experimentation and practice. Unlike *After Virtue's* ostensibly pessimistic view, the perspective here in "After Teaching" is one of jubilant expectation that our post-Enlightenment crises will either force new cultures of consensus, or create dissenting cultures that will serve as survivor traditions for the next century.

II

> If the physicians and the lawyers and the architects and the engineers and ultimately all citizens shared a general education in common, it is just possible they could talk to one another and to the rest of us about matters of common and pressing concern, a sort of discussion which is manifestly impossible under present circumstances.
>
> —*Three Dialogues on Liberal Education*[7]

One can recognize a recurrent motif in the culture analyses of Alasdair MacIntyre: Enlightenment traditions disintegrate the classical and religious heritage of Western civilization, without providing an alternative worldview as a precondition for ethical consensus and coherent social-political formations. The impossibility of consensus on issues involving moral practice, social justice, and political action is the result of our inherited inability to find common criteria for negotiating the conflicts that arise from differing perspectives. This scenario of fragmented ethical criteria inherited from our Enlightenment past frames MacIntyre's critique not only of modern ethics but also of modern education. Consider one of several culture forecasts, typical of his reflection on modern ethics, but focused here on modern education. In this passage MacIntyre argues that the two traditional goals of Western education, preparing students for future occupations and preparing them to think for themselves, have become mutually exclusive:

> [I]t is only where there is an educated public that [these two] central aims of all modern educational systems can be compatibly pursued. . . . [W]here we have so far believed that our teachers could pursue both these aims . . . we should have instead to conclude first that a certain kind of failure is inherent in modern educational systems, a kind of failure that no type of educational reform can be expected to remedy, and secondly that in respect of these two aims teachers confront not a both/and, but an either/or.[8]

According to MacIntyre, the precondition for combining our two otherwise disjunct educational goals consists in the capacity to create and sustain an educated public. Only such a public, he argues, can insure a coherence between the educational objectives of liberal learning on the

one hand, and societal expectations on the other. That is, only an educated public would continue to value, endorse, and make available "the
kind of social roles and occupation for which a given educational system
is training the young . . . [roles and occupations whose] exercise requires, or is at least compatible with, the possession of a general culture . . . [and which would] enable each young person to think for
him or herself." But the existence of an educated public that can cooperate in sustaining such coherence, MacIntyre declares, is yet another one
of those casualties of Europe's eighteenth-century Enlightenment project. The atrophy or stillbirth of an educated public is attributed by Mac-
Intyre to the "self-dissolving" culture of the Enlightenment. It was
a culture shaped by thinkers, statesmen, and a rising bourgeoisie who
undermined their ability to endow succeeding generations with their
own civic freedoms and industrial opportunities. "The protagonists of
growth, development and largeness of scale in state and economy were
engendering a type of society in which they themselves would no longer
be possible."[9] I will turn to a spiritual dimension of this Enlightenment
self-dissolution momentarily. But first it is necessary to question
MacIntyre's representations of the kind of educated public that is prerequisite to a unified achievement of our two educational objectives.

What is meant by the phrase, "educated public"? As if to acknowledge his own biased use of the phrase, MacIntyre confesses our collective captivity to Enlightenment presuppositions about the nature of
knowledge and the purpose of education. First he states in characteristic
fashion a strong negative: "the concept of an educated public has no way
of taking on life in contemporary society. It is at most a ghost haunting
our educational systems." But then he hints, without taking seriously
the option to seize an alternative perspective, that we ourselves may
need to be "exorcised" or liberated from this ghostly concept.

> Nonetheless it is a ghost that cannot be exorcised. Our inheritance from the
> culture of the Enlightenment is so pervasive that we cannot rid ourselves of
> attitudes to the arts and sciences which presuppose that introduction into
> membership of an educated public of at least some of our pupils is one of the
> central aims of our educational systems.[10]

What would an alternative attitude to the arts and sciences presuppose? In responding to that query I turn to a typology of knowledge and learning that is more comprehensive than that afforded by MacIntyre's rationalist approach or his textual, canonic and literacy emphases.[11]

While discussing Christian theological traditions, Catholic theologian Robert Schreiter presents four cognitive approaches that can also apply to Western cognitive traditions in general, both oral and literary. Cognitive approaches generally, like theological knowledge specifically, can also be categorized by Schreiter's fourfold typology: (1) variations on a (sacred) text—commentaries, narratives, and anthologies; (2) wisdom or *sapientia*—oral traditions of proverbs or aphoristic sayings on the one hand, and manuals, instructional treatises, and mystical writings on the other; (3) sure knowledge or *scientia*—analytic and systematic presentations and treatises; and (4) *praxis*—social analysis, ideology critique, and reflection on action (or practice in concert with theory).[12] Whereas MacIntyre's discussion of education seems to highlight types 1 and 3, in this chapter I am most concerned with types 2 and 4: the wisdom or sapiential cognitive forms most evident in oral cultures and traditions, and the praxial modes of reflection most pertinent to cultures of victimization or oppression. Elsewhere Schreiter contrasts praxis as a focus of cognitive processes with a fifth category, what he calls "ethnographic" approaches as distinguished from "liberation" approaches. Ethnographic approaches focus on cultural and religious identity, whereas liberation approaches (theologies of praxis) seek social transformation.[13] The best possibility of course, as Schreiter himself acknowledges, is to allow due attention to all the modes of human cognitive excellence—a challenge that I attempt to meet in the remainder of this study.

III

I recall taking undergraduate philosophy classes in the 1960's in which Plato and Socrates were taught without reference to the fact that they were contemplative mystics who believed in immortality and reincarnation.
—*Robert N. Sollod, "The Hollow Curriculum"*[14]

For Greek philosophers the primacy of reason was balanced by other cognitive inclinations. Those inclinations derived from a vital wisdom tradition, and were conveyed by an oral culture still infused with its mythic or cosmological vision of the world. Language philosopher Walter Ong reminds us of this wisdom tradition in his studies of orality and literacy.

> Despite the fact that Plato's philosophy . . . was the product of literacy, Plato . . . calculatingly used the dialogue form to give the teachings something like their original oral cast, protesting in his Seventh Letter that one cannot put what is really essential to wisdom in writing, for this is to falsify it, and noting in the *Phaedrus* (274) that writing serves merely recall, not memory or wisdom.[15]

While they emphasized the preeminence of reason in their reflections, ancient thinkers did not feel compelled to subordinate the wisdom traditions of their indigenous culture. However, in the modern period the desire for cognitive certainty and the demand for a linear logic conducive to precision in analytic and technical writing has resulted in widespread devaluing of the legitimacy of other modes of knowing.

The devaluation of extra-rational or nondiscursive ends and means is not a necessary feature of modernity, however. Contemporary non-Western peoples who have not experienced Europe's Enlightenment conditioning evince more diversified and inclusive modes of rational development and technological progress. In this regard the German theologian Dietrich Bonhoeffer marveled that technology in Asia "acquires a totally different significance [than in the West] in that it ceases to be an end in itself. Technical development in the Islamic world, for example, continues to stand entirely in the service of belief in God and of the constructive furtherance of Islamic history."[16] Such a correlation of technology and spirituality leads me to return to Robert Schreiter's treatment of the wisdom traditions of oral and traditional cultures. Schreiter's treatment is commendable here because he highlights the wisdom and praxial interests of cultures that are typically overlooked by liberal education, and because he avoids subordinating their cognitive traditions either to textualist or to scientific approaches. Wisdom traditions from ancient Greece to contemporary developing nations display one of the features which Schreiter highlights also for wisdom traditions in Christian cultures. That feature is the "cosmoscopic" imperative "to see the world, both the visible and the invisible, as a unified whole."[17]

In Western philosophical and religious traditions this imperative is expressed in the impulse to hold together distinct domains of knowledge: knowledge of nature (natural sciences), knowledge of humanity (human sciences), and knowledge of divinity (theological sciences). The premier classical example is the works of Aristotle, as a compendium of all the disciplines of his age (for which achievement he is acknowledged, in medieval or Thomistic parlance, as "the philosopher"). The Western tradition of liberal education inherits this philosophical wholism, in which the attainment of wisdom (Greek: *philosophia,* love of wisdom) is the end or *telos* of lifelong learning. However, wisdom does not consist in mastery of all the parts (for example, understanding all the natural and human sciences as well as theology or religious studies), but rather in understanding the particulars sufficiently to know how they are ordered as elements of a whole. The inheritance of this wisdom perspective in contemporary liberal studies programs can be seen in the following comment from William Darkey:

> Liberal education in the proper sense is concerned with the whole range of human knowledge and of human experience . . . is concerned with *wholes,* with *genera.* For this reason it is a very different thing from any specialized discipline and also from any agglomeration of such disciplines, for these are by definition concerned with *species.* . . . It is perfectly obvious, for example, that ethics, poetry, politics, science and mathematics have profoundly important relationships to one another, and yet their normal curricular disposition tends to insulate them from each other.[18]

It is precisely this wisdom imperative to comprehend discrete domains of knowledge and experience in a unified vision of the whole (the universe) that Western cultures forfeited in their Enlightenment rationalism. In the Enlightenment project of the seventeenth and eighteenth centuries, rationalism was extracted from all other cognitive processes for its evident power to provide reliable forms of apodictic (demonstrated) knowledge. The deep desire or will to power of Western thinkers, in formal philosophy as well as in the empirical sciences, was directed toward a rationalist conquest of "the unthought"—to borrow the term of the twentieth-century French philosopher, Michel Foucault. I take Foucault's term to connote an alienated condition, in which human knowledge exists as an isolated construct "surrounded on all sides by an immense region of shadow in which labour, life, and language conceal their truth (and their origin) from those very beings who speak, who exist, and who are at work."[19] This view of humanity's cognitive situation is intolerable for the modern temper, which is obsessed with an unending project: to convert the unthought into the thought in ever-widening domains of investigation and control. In postmodern retrospect we are now able to distance ourselves from, and thus to appraise critically, this Cartesian quest to reduce the range of the unthought and the uncontrolled as much as possible.

More conducive to the trajectory of this chapter is an interest in retrieving wisdom traditions that esteem rationality but preclude compulsive rationalism. Such traditions accept uncertainty, mystery, or indeterminacy as a matter of course—as ingredient in, or constitutive of, both material and spiritual realities of human experience. In these traditions the cognitive task is not to jettison the indeterminate and the extra-rational, but to mediate its engagement with the rational in diverse projects requiring a unified vision of the world and of human experience.

Alongside such traditions I now juxtapose Alasdair MacIntyre's concluding counsel to teachers engaged in liberal learning. He advises them that, in the absence of an educated public capable of bridging the occupational and the intellectual objectives of education, they must reinvent the kind of communities necessary to foster their wholistic objectives. To this counsel he also adds a curricular item almost as an afterthought:

Such teachers would therefore have to ask themselves how that kind of community is to be reinvented. Where could they look for answers?

. . . [A] revival of the reading of Greek philosophical and political texts would necessarily be central to any form of education that could enable a community to resist this outcome [the demise of an educated public] successfully or to recover from it.[20]

I, too, would call for a revival of the reading of classical Greek texts. But first I would expand my selection beyond the conventional philosophical and political texts to Greek tragedies, poetry, and myth. Then I would balance and diversify the hermeneutic (interpretive) appropriation of this literature, to emphasize its wisdom and mythopoeic dimensions alongside the rational and discursive. My hermeneutic predisposition of interpretive communities would be shaped in part by the perspectives of such works as F. M. Cornford's *Principium Sapientiae: The Origins of Greek Philosophical Thought* (an examination of the origins of Greek philosophy in ancient shamanism), and E. R. Dodds's *The Greeks and The Irrational.*[21] Finally, I would also—as a matter of intrinsic intellectual merit—extend my textual field to encompass texts from other ancient literary traditions that similarly display *sapientia* and *scientia* as complementary realms of human cognitive skill and excellence. Such an extension would comprise a broad selection of cultures and their histories, thus converging with the subject-matter of recent multicultural curricula. But rather than replacing traditional curricula comprising the Western classics with multicultural subjects, I insist on interconnecting the two. Accordingly, I would correlate Greek and Roman classics with other classical texts of the ancient Mediterranean world and the Middle East (Egypt, Israel, Babylonia), as well as India, Persia, and China. I would also include the contemporary literatures of African and African American, Asian and Asian American, Hispanic, and South American peoples, according due attention to gender, class, and related differences in the literary expression of those cultures.

A limited selection of such correlations must suffice here by way of illustration. Consider the Breuer-Telson stage and video production of "The Gospel at Colonus."[22] The viewer is impressed by its remarkable fidelity both to Sophocles' original Greek version of *Oedipus at Colonus,* and to the spirituality of black North American Pentecostal church traditions. In this conveyance of an ancient text by means of contemporary multimedia, director Lee Breuer has adapted Sophocles' *Oedipus at Colonus* using the Robert Fitzgerald translation, and incorporated passages from the other two plays in the Oedipus cycle: *Oedipus Rex* and *Antigone*. The production's musical director, Bob Telson, has composed and arranged songs for black gospel music singers and a mass choir that portray the characters and the chorus of the original play. But it is notable that the arrangements are improvisational in modes consistent with Afro-American musical traditions in jazz and the blues. In those traditions, performances do not merely repeat their sources but dynamically transform them. The result, therefore, is authentically Afro-American; at the same time, the viewer is thoroughly engaged and encompassed by the ancient world of Sophocles' text. The common element that enables such a remarkable fusion of the two worlds, ancient Greek and contemporary African American, is the ecstatic dimension of religious experience. What the viewer learns in the correlation of these two culture texts is that the estatic condition is essentially co-extensive with human existence in diverse cultures.[23]

Other correlations of black studies and Western classics include Plato's *Crito* and Martin Luther King Jr.'s *Letter from a Birmingham Jail* ("Socrates and King in Jail"); Augustine's *Confessions* and *The Autobiography of Malcolm X* (each about a profligate youth who is converted, reforms, and rises to religious leadership, Christian and Black Muslim respectively); Euripides' *Medea* and Toni Morrison's *Beloved* (each about a woman who murders her offspring).[24] Yet such multicultural correlations are not brought about through a liberal democratic ideology of parity for its own sake. These examples of black studies materials and conventional classics reflect the academic interests of this chapter to encompass in a wholistic vision our composite experience and heritage as Westerners, not a kind of liberal politicization of the curriculum (as in Clausewitz's description of politics as "warfare by other means"[25]).

I have indicated in limited terms how such a wholistic participation in both classical and contemporary cultures might be designed in terms of a curriculum of correlations in black studies. Other models are possible, of course, and they would extend to fields involving not only black studies and western studies, but also other ethnic studies in correlation with conventional arts and sciences curricula. Toward this programmatic goal I propose a 'multicentric' (compare 'Eurocentric' and 'Afrocentric') model of intercultural correlation: a field theory of multiple centers for correlating Western classics with the expressions of human excellence produced by non-Western and marginalized cultures.

IV

The larger conclusion is that since specialization is necessary and proper for the acquisition of professional skills, liberal education is an absolutely essential preparation for professional studies in order that the professions do not become blind and isolated practices.

—*Three Dialogues on Liberal Education*[26]

Today's crisis of academic professionalism resembles the nineteenth-century transition in the United States from educators who were professional clergy to educators as an accredited professoriate. "Just as the schools were secularized when the clergy's professional impulse no longer served a more general need, so today it may well be that academicians can no longer offer an appropriate education to a still broader generality of students through a range of formal apprenticeships to professional scholars."[27] Today the professoriate may be experiencing its own version of clerical dysfunction, in which the professional interests and rigors of an educating class prove to be too specialized, myopic, and constricting for the needs and requirements of a general public. General education is at risk from the side of academia itself, in the form of a professoriate that appears incapable of attending to education in the public interest because of absorption in education for its own professional interests. "Trained as specialists to train other specialists, sought and judged as specialists, . . . college professors seem decreasingly inclined or even able to organize and offer the broad, liberal education of late adolescents." A programmatic turn to oral traditions and to multicultural studies may be able to remedy this deformation of liberal learning, but at the level of praxis as much as curriculum content.[28]

On this point I favor the critique of "the age of academe" offered by Russell Jacoby, a critique which differs from Alasdair MacIntyre's view of the atrophy of an educated public. Jacoby locates the crisis of education at the opposite end of the spectrum. He admits, on the one hand, that the American public who eagerly read Thomas Paine during the colonial period, for example, or who later endured hours of debates by Abraham Lincoln and Stephen Douglas, no longer exists. But he resists a simple comparison. "A reading public may be no more . . . but [that] is not the whole truth." Rather than blame the public (compare "blaming the victim"), Jacoby correlates the state of public education with the state of public intellectuals:

> A public that reads serious books, magazines, and newspapers has dwindled; it has not vanished. The writings of older intellectuals from John Kenneth Galbraith to Daniel Bell continue to elicit interest and discussion. . . . The audience may be contracting, but younger intellectuals are missing. That is the emphasis here, less on the eclipse of a public than on the eclipse of public intellectuals.[29]

In *The Last Intellectuals*—his requiem for a passing era of publicly engaged and engaging scholars—Jacoby proceeds to trace the absorption of American intellectuals into academic institutions from the 1950s to the present. The result was the virtual withdrawal of scholars from the forums and media that had provided public arenas for earlier generations. Jacoby is certainly aware that intellectuals were not free agents in that transformation: "To live from selling book reviews and articles ceased to be difficult; it became impossible. The number of serious magazines and newspapers steadily declined . . . leaving few avenues; the signs all pointed toward the colleges. . . . After this decade [1950s] intellectuals joined established institutions or retrained." Nevertheless, Jacoby is critical of the acquiescence of "New Left" professors in their institutional isolation from the public realm: "That it is difficult for an educated adult American to name a single political scientist or sociologist or philosopher is not wholly his or her fault; the professionals have abandoned the public arena. The influx of left scholars has not changed the picture; reluctantly or enthusiastically they gain respectability at the cost of identity." Irrespective of their own constraints within a culture that requires that they find employment in accredited institutions, scholars are nonetheless to be held accountable for their cooptation by such institutions—their functional (however reluctant or enthusiastic) collusion in "setting up private clubs for accredited members."[30]

Jacoby's call for an alternative public role for scholars converges with MacIntyre's call for teachers to create alternative communities that redress the deficiencies of an educated public. Both could benefit from an opportunity that is emerging in this study: an opportunity at the level of praxis rather than theory or intellection alone. This is the opportunity for professionals themselves to become co-learners with their students and their public. In the preceding section I framed this opportunity in terms of a multicultural classics curriculum that is inclusive of cognitive styles and approaches across the spectrum, from textual and scientific-philosophical to oral and wisdom traditions. In this section we can appreciate that such an innovation conveys a praxis that is the precise negation of the academy's current institutional hegemony over the nation's educational life. The profound reorientation of the academy that such co-learning would entail suggests one way to account for the resistance that multicultural curricula encounter. Professional instructors, grounded as they are in their scholarly expertise and control over a reasonably defined subject matter within a limited discipline, are understandably reluctant to jeopardize that expertise by embracing new materials and agendas that stretch conventional configurations of their disciplines. Many are also, we can reasonably suspect, daunted by the prospect of learning new materials alongside their students, thus becoming, to some extent, their peers.

To a certain degree such instructors are right to anticipate in multiculturalism the threat or promise of an end to academic departmentalization as we know it. However, that prospect can be coopted in all-too-familiar academic fashion, and in a manner that would effectively abort the relationship of instructor and student as co-learners (at the cost of the egalitarian transformation offered by co-learning). For multicultural classics can be introduced into conventional curricula merely to provide new

materials for the same methodologies that privilege *scientia* traditions and
textualist approaches, that neglect wisdom traditions and their implications for new forms of praxis, and that maintain the standard hierarchical
relationship between instructors and their students. What this cooptation
would forfeit is the opportunity to render instructors and students as
peer subjects of materials in relation to which they are both irreducibly
learners and, optimally, co-learners.

V

> Incomprehensibly, traditionalists who oppose adding multicultural content
> to the curriculum also ignore the religious and theological bases of the
> Western civilization that they seek to defend.
> —*Robert N. Sollod, "The Hollow Curriculum"*[31]

An antidote to the reductionist attitude toward traditional curricula
described above consists in the multicultural innovations that some tra-
ditionalists eschew. "Today's advocates of Western traditionalism focus,
for the most part, on conveying a type of rationalism that is only a single
strain in Western thought." A multiculturalism that included the religion and spirituality of its subjects would, by implication, address the
academy's myopia with respect to its traditional subjects of study. However, the one-dimensional or rationalist focus operating in conventional
curricula can also deform multicultural studies.

> Multiculturalism that does not include appreciation of the deepest visions of
> reality reminds me of the travelogues that I saw in the cinema as a child—full
> of details of quaint and somewhat mysterious behavior that evoked some
> superficial empathy but no real, in-depth understanding. Implicit in a multi-
> cultural approach that ignores spiritual factors is a . . . patronizing atti-
> tude. It assumes that we can understand and evaluate the experiences of other
> cultures without comprehension of their deepest beliefs.[32]

On the one hand, as Sollod maintains a multiculturalism that avoids
consideration of the religious perspectives and the characteristic spiritual-
ities of the cultures studied is ineffectual. Yet multicultural studies that

revitalize traditional curricula would be misappropriated if they relegated the treatment of religion and spirituality to the study of non-Western or marginalized cultures, and did not recognize the centrality of religion and spirituality across all cultures. "It is difficult to imagine, for example, how ethical issues can be intelligently approached and discussed or how wise ethical decisions can be reached without either knowledge or reference to those religious and spiritual principles that underlie our legal system and moral codes."[33]

This observation is penultimate to the final focus of this chapter: the reintegration of the occupational-professional and the critical-cultural objectives of education. We have considered multicultural curricula and the wisdom traditions in which a wholism operates (for example) between the cognitive imperatives of rationality on the one hand, and mythopoeic and religious interests on the other. In concluding the chapter we turn to narratives that are able to integrate such disparate realms as the occupational-professional and the critical-cultural. Narrative forms of cognitive processing, like wisdom cognitive traditions, have been devalued in modern academic institutions.[34] But it is precisely through their stories that most persons and cultures process the relationship between their everyday existence and their highest ideals. In this regard "we are constantly striving, with more or less success, to occupy the story-tellers' position with respect to our own lives." Failure to attend to the narrative formation of human understanding deprives students and the public generally of their most natural resource for integrating the goals of liberal learning with the goal of making a living. In this connection Stephen Crites, in "The Narrative Quality of Experience," and David Carr, in "Narrative and the Real World: An Argument for Continuity," have argued that narrative construals are not artificial or lower order forms of cognition. Narrative is not an elementary framework which should be jettisoned in preference for more abstract forms as one's reasoning powers become more sophisticated. Rather, "narrative structure pervades our very experience of time and social existence . . . [as] the structure inherent in human experience and action."[35]

The turn to narrative complements the turn to wisdom, which indeed is often expressed in non-narrative forms (such as proverbs and

aphorisms, as noted above).[36] But together these complementary approaches offer the possibility of transcending the academic professionalism which renders instruction self-serving and narrowly specialized.
Whereas wisdom studies are conducive to a multicultural expansion of
conventional curricula, attention to the narrative formation of student
learning correlates with the public context within which that learning
occurs. For narrative provides the most publicly accessible form for formulating, organizing, and expressing cognitive content. The academy's
current devaluation of narrative, with its preference for abstruse formu-
lations of theory and scholarly references, implicitly excludes the public
as audience and participant in academic discourse. The neglect of narrative modes of formulating ideas insures that students for whom those
modes are most congenial (a majority of students?) will be impoverished
in their retention of academic content and processes. Finally, it insures
that the instructional event itself will be a one-sided performance, in
which the instructor (better schooled in theory, information, and scho-
lasticism) plays such a dominant role that students remain passive specta-
tors rather than peer participants in the learning process.

The lament that prefaced this chapter, "I did a terrible thing today, I
taught a class," can be a proper response to pedagogies that displace each
student's responsible participation in the learning process in her or his
own right. I have proposed that wisdom orientations and multicultural
curricula can serve to moderate the excesses of professional expertise
among instructors, rendering them co-learners with their students in
terms of content. Similarly, the restoration of narrative as instructional
discourse can insure that modes of learning remain publicly accessible,
accountable, and intelligible. But finally, it remains true for many in the
teaching profession that the most fulfilling experience "after teaching" is
the sense that one has participated in a process that transcends the self-
interests of one's own career, institution, or discipline. In this regard,
perhaps the most comprehensive framework for the teaching experience
in Western and non-Western cultures alike is a spiritually-configured
narrative. It is the story of the wise teacher whose objective is to mediate
the ability of students to apprehend for themselves realities that fuse
the everyday with the extraordinary—with God, or knowledge, or the

truth, or beauty, or love, or the good, or the just. If contemporary education requires forfeiting the narrative framework of learning as initiation into such wisdom, then the prospect for "after teaching" is terrible indeed. Let us insure that it need not be so.

NOTES

1. I read or heard this quotation in the form of a remark by a St. John's College "tutor" or professor. St. John's (my *alma mater*), has campuses in Annapolis, Maryland and Santa Fe, New Mexico, and is a small liberal arts school distinguished by its "great books" curriculum of Western classics in the humanities and sciences.

2. Again, St. John's College provides a useful source here:

> St. John's faculty members do not teach in the usual sense. We seem like very strange professors. Actually we are not professors at all. We are "tutors".
> . . . My job as a tutor is not to teach subject matter. It is to encourage the growth of a habit. I sit around the table with my students. I am not there as an academic authority. This would put intellectual responsibility solely in my hands. It belongs in theirs. . . . Specialized training [in contrast to liberal education] requires a different kind of college, one in which the teacher functions as an expert who is there to give information to the would-be expert who does not yet have it. . . . Specialized education must be taught. I do not believe that a college can be both a teaching institution and a community of learning. St. John's has chosen to be the latter.

"A Tutor's Comment," promotional brochure of St. John's College, Annapolis, Maryland and Santa Fe, New Mexico. By contrast with this purist expression of liberal learning, conventional academic institutions in the United States attempt both liberal and specialized education simultaneously—with widely varying degrees of success and failure. In this chapter I have attempted to hold the two goals together, while being fully aware of the tensions involved.

3. "Statement of the St. John's Program, 1990–1991," *St. John's College Catalog 1990–1991* (Annapolis, MD and Santa Fe, NM, 1990), 6.

4. Stanley Hauerwas, with Richard Bondi and David B. Burrell, *Truthfulness and Tragedy* (Notre Dame, IN: University of Notre Dame Press, 1977), 10.

5. On the term "culture texts" see Robert J. Schreiter, *Constructing Local Theologies* (Maryknoll, NY: Orbis Books, 1985), 55: "While the word

'text' comes from linguistics, texts are both verbal and nonverbal phenomena, which can bear a message and thus serve as the basic unit of investigation. Paul Ricoeur, in a different context, has elaborated something of the same idea. Thus a text can be a set of words, an event, or even a person. Culture then becomes the total sum of these texts shared by a given people." (Cf. 29–31, 61–73.)

My own existential quest for psychosocial wholeness finds most eloquent expression in a classic text in black studies by W. E. B. Du Bois. See *The Souls of Black Folk* (1903) in *W. E. B. Du Bois: Writings* (New York: The Library of America, 1986). This celebrated passage, with its obvious implications for my dual proposals in this chapter (both liberal arts traditionalist and multicultural) merit quotation here (364–65):

> It is a peculiar sensation, this double-consciousness, this sense of always looking at one's self through the eyes of others, of measuring one's soul by the tape of a world that looks on in amused contempt and pity. One ever feels his two-ness— an American, a Negro; two souls, two thoughts, two unreconciled strivings; two warring ideals in one dark body, whose dogged strength alone keeps it from being torn asunder.
>
> The history of the American Negro is the history of this strife—this longing to attain self-conscious manhood, to merge his double self into a better and truer self. In this merging he wishes neither of the older selves to be lost. He would not Africanize America [cf. Afrocentrism], for America has too much to teach the world and Africa. He would not bleach his Negro soul in flood of white Americanism [cf. Eurocentrism], for he knows that Negro blood has a message for the world. He simply wishes to make it possible for a man to be both a Negro and an American.

6. Alasdair MacIntyre, *After Virtue: A Study in Moral Theory,* 2nd ed., (Notre Dame, IN: University of Notre Dame Press, 1984).

7. William A. Darkey, ed., *Three Dialogues on Liberal Education* (Annapolis, MD: The St. John's College Press, 1979), 122.

8. "Either [teachers] can continue to pursue the aim of fitting their pupils for the type and level of social role and occupation prescribed in their society for the products of that part of the educational system in which they are at work [their speciality], or they can continue to pursue the aim of enabling their pupils to think for themselves, but they cannot coherently pursue both aims." Alasdair MacIntyre, "The Idea of an Educated Public," *Education and Values,* ed. Graham Haydon (London: Institute of Education, University of London, 1987), 34.

9. Ibid., 16, 35. "The success of Hume and Adam Smith . . . produced a society in which the type of culture of which Hume and Adam Smith were so distinguished a part became impossible" (p. 35).

10. Ibid., 34.

11. MacIntyre's rationalist and textualist criteria for the existence of an educated public comprise three areas: (1) "There must first of all be a tolerably large body of individuals, educated into both the habit and the opportunity of active rational debate. . . . " (2) "A second type of requirement is shared assent, both to the standards by appeal to which the success or failure of any particular thesis or argument is to be judged, and to the form of rational justification from which those standards derive their authority." (3) There must be "some large degree of shared background beliefs and attitudes, informed by the widespread reading of a common body of texts, texts which are accorded a canonical status. . . ." Ibid., 18–19.

12. Schreiter, *Constructing Local Theologies,* p. 86. Examples in terms of theological and other literary sources include: (1) *variations on a sacred text:* commentaries (e.g., Mishnah and Talmud in Judaism, *hadith* literature in Islam, Vendanta literature in Hinduism—i.e., variations on the Vedas—and commentaries on the sutras in Buddhism and on the scriptures in Christianity); narratives, most notably hagiographies (stories of saints and holy persons) and martyrologies, but also including noncanonical literature (e.g., apocryphal stories) and personal narratives; (2) *wisdom or sapientia:* proverbs, both oral and literary (e.g., the biblical proverbs presented as the "wisdom" of Solomon), and other aphoristic forms (from folk sayings to Pascal's *Pensees* or Nietzsche's *Thus Spake Zarathustra*), as well as instructional manuals, treatises, and mystical writings (e.g., gnostic texts, the writings of St. John of the Cross, or Kahlil Gibran's *The Prophet*); (3) *sure knowledge or scientia:* apologetic treatises or disputations, scholastic argumentation and systematic works, analytic writings and critiques, all expressed in "the most exact form of knowledge known to the culture" (e.g., Aquinas' *Summa,* Spinoza's *Tractatus,* Calvin's *Institutes*); (4) *praxis:* social analysis and ideology critiques, and community as well as theoretical reflection on action (e.g., liberation theologies based on Marxist analysis; and civil rights, human rights, or freedom movements based on folk or religious traditions).

13. Ibid., 13f. Intriguingly, Schreiter describes liberation theologies as "wisdom theologies turned outward," and wisdom theologies conversely as the pursuit of "reflection and action via the interior path" (p. 93).

14. Robert N. Sollod, "The Hollow Curriculum," *The Chronicle of Higher Education* 38:28 (March 18, 1992), A60.

15. "By the time writing has the hold it achieved among the ancient Greeks, something like a vision of a neutral [objective] world is largely arrived at, even though the universe is still shot through with animism, as in Aristotle's living celestial spheres." Walter J. Ong, *The Presence of the Word* (New Haven and London: Yale University Press, 1967), 55, 224; cf. Walter J. Ong, *Orality and Literacy* (London and New York: Methuen, 1982), Eric A. Havelock, *Preface to Plato* (Cambridge, MA: Harvard University Press, 1963), and *The Muse Learns to Write: Reflections on Orality and Literacy from Antiquity to the Present* (New Haven and London: Yale University Press, 1986).

16. Dietrich Bonhoeffer, *Ethics,* trans. Neville Horton Smith (New York: The Macmillan Co., 1961), 35. In the West, by contrast: "Emancipated reason rose to unsuspected heights. . . . Reason became a working hypothesis, a heuristic principle, and so led on to the unparalleled rise of technology . . . [to] something essentially new in the history of the world. From the Egyptian pyramids and the Greek temples to the medieval cathedrals and the eighteenth century, technology had always been a matter of artisanship. It stood in the service of religion, of kings, of art, and of the daily needs of men. The technical science of the modern western world has emancipated itself from any kind of subservience. It is in essence not service but mastery . . . an entirely new spirit . . . the spirit of the forcible subjugation of nature beneath the rule of the thinking and experimenting man" (pp. 34–35).

17. Schreiter, *Constructing Local Theologies,* 86.

18. Darkey, *Three Dialogues on Liberal Education,* 120. "[Even] 'interdepartmental' or 'cross-disciplinary' programs . . . rarely consist of more than a variety of specialized elective courses which were never conceived as having any integral relation to one another or in which there is an ordering principle of wholeness. Of course, if the student can discover any such relationships for himself, so much the better, but it is not conceived to be the college's responsibility to help him do so."

19. Michel Foucault, *The Order of Things: An Archaeology of the Human Sciences* (New York: Random House, 1970), 331; and in *After Foucault: Humanistic Knowledge, Postmodern Challenges,* ed. Jonathan Arac (New Brunswick and London: Rutgers University Press, 1988), p. 17.

20. MacIntyre, "The Idea of An Educated Public," 34–35. Despite his curricular prescription, MacIntyre eschews a reading of his essay as "even in part a call for curricular reform . . . [which] may on other grounds be a good or a bad thing" (p. 33). It is on such "other grounds" that I offer my own curricular prescriptions in this chapter.

21. F. M. Cornford, *Principium Sapientiae: The Origins of Greek Philosophical Thought* (New York: Harper & Row, 1965). E. R. Dodds, *The Greeks and The Irrational* (Berkeley: University of California Press, 1951). Cf. also Henri Frankfort and Henrietta A. Groenewegen-Frankfort, *Before Philosophy: An Essay on Speculative Thought in the Ancient Near East* (Baltimore: Penguin Books, 1954).

22. "The Gospel at Colonus," directed by Lee Breuer and Bob Telson, original production by Brooklyn Academy of Music, Inc., 1983. For distribution see Princeton: Films for the Humanities, Inc., 1988.

23. Cf. I. M. Lewis, *Ecstatic Religion: A Study of Shamanism and Spirit Possession* (London and New York: Routledge, 1989), and Mircea Eliade, *Shamanism: Archaic Techniques of Esctasy* (London: Routledge, 1970).

24. The first two entries in this paragraph are courses that have been offered by Professor Winston Van Horne at the University of Wisconsin–Milwaukee. The third is a course offered by Professor William Cook at Dartmouth University. A formal, programmatic statement of such correlations, including other illustrations, is available from the author in (currently) unpublished form under the title, "Improvisational Black Studies: A Field Theory Approach."

25. Cf. David Bromwich, *Politics By Other Means: Higher Education and Group Thinking* (New Haven: Yale University Press, 1992).

26. Darkey, *Three Dialogues on Liberal Education,* 122. "Liberal education in one aspect may be said to concern itself with the consideration of ends, of means towards ends, and of the relationships of ends and means. Graduate (or professional) education, on the other hand, is with equal propriety concerned with means alone, appropriate particular ends having been presumed by the discipline itself. To recognize this is to grasp the full sense in which liberal or general education is prior to professional or specialized education. The two are complementary to one another and are never in competition except when they become confused and try to usurp one another's functions. . . . [Thus] as long ago as Aristotle, the . . . principle was enunciated

that the arts, or what we term practices and professions, do not judge of their own ends (p. 121).

27. *16 to 20: The Liberal Education of an Age Group,* by the Four-School Study Committee (New York: The College Entrance Examination Board, 1970), 31f.

28. Ibid., 4. On academic professionalism from the side of liberal learning, MacIntyre laments the following deformation of the academy:

> When Kant enjoined us to think for ourselves, it could never have occurred to him that thinking, in the sense in which he was talking about it, might be deformed into a professionalized activity, largely unavailable except in specialized contents. Yet just this is what has happened in modern society. Thinking has become the occupational responsibility of those who discharge certain social roles: the professional scientist, for example. But those topics thinking about which is of general social concern . . . not only in literature, but also in politics and economics, *either* are handed over to certain disciplined, but limited because professionalized, specialists, *or* are dealt with in forums in which the constraints of disciplined exchange are almost entirely lacking. MacIntyre, "The Idea of an Educated Public" (p. 25).

29. Russell Jacoby, *The Last Intellectuals: American Culture in the Age of Academe* (New York: Noonday Press/Farrar, Straus and Giroux, 1987), 6. Jacoby focuses this critique in a chapter devoted entirely to "New Left" intellectuals.

> The New Left sprang into life around and against universities; its revulsion seemed visceral. Yet New Left intellectuals became professors who neither looked backward nor sideways; they kept their eyes on professional journals, monographs, and conferences. Perhaps because their lives had unfolded almost entirely on campuses they were unable or unwilling to challenge academic imperatives. . . . [Their scholarship] is largely technical, unreadable and—except by specialists—unread . . . more and more like the work it sought to subvert. . . . In the end it was not the New Left intellectuals who invaded the universities but the reverse: the academic idiom, concepts, and concerns occupied, and finally preoccupied, young left intellectuals" (pp. 140–41).

The apparent discrepancy between Jacoby's critique and that of a more recent work, Roger Kimball's *Tenured Radicals: How Politics Has Corrupted Our Higher Education* (New York: Harper & Row, 1990), may be explained by observing the largely insular nature of campus radicalism which still manages to avoid the public arena despite its rhetoric of social activism and emancipatory praxis.

30. Ibid., 19, 190. Another observer similarly remarks: "Conceding the [detrimental] tilt toward research at universities, some faculty members have suggested that it was imposed by administrators seeking to enhance the prestige of their institutions. Those faculty members now assert that a harmonious balance once existed between teaching and research, a balance that administrations could restore. But this supposition is questionable. . . . [Administrators] have bought into the value system that attaches prestige mainly to research reputations and the amount of grant money received. But it is the faculties that spawned the research culture and maintain it through hiring and tenure practices that they control." Bryan Barnett, "Teaching and Research Are Inescapably Incompatible," *The Chronicle of Higher Education* XXXVIII:39 (June 3, 1992), A40.

31. Sollod, "The Hollow Curriculum," p. A60.

32. Ibid.

33. Ibid.

34. "By teaching us to prefer a 'principle' or a 'rational' description to a narrative description, the standard account not only fails to account for the significance of narrative but also . . . fails to provide us with the critical skills to know the limits of the narrative which currently has us in its grasp . . . [for example] the narrative born of the Enlightenment. The plot was given in capsule by Auguste Comte: first came religion in the form of stories, then philosophy in the form of metaphysical analysis, and then science with its exact methods. . . . Hegel [in another story] shows us how each of these ages supplanted the other as a refinement in the progressive development of reason. So stories are prescientific, according to the story legitimizing the age which calls itself scientific." Stanley Hauerwas, *Truthfulness and Tragedy* (Notre Dame, IN: University of Notre Dame Press, 1977), 25.

35. David Carr, in "Narrative and the Real World: An Argument for Continuity," *History and Theory* XXV:2 (1986): 125; and Carr, *Time, Narrative, and History* (Bloomington: Indiana University Press, 1986), 9, 65.

36. In an excursus on biblical hermeneutics the philosopher Paul Ricoeur has noted both the divergence and the convergence of biblical narrative and wisdom literature.

> I am first of all struck by the way in which the proverbs, in spite of their modesty, conjoin in a striking way the everyday and the immemorial. The everyday is the time of works and days. It is punctuated by those maxims that tell how to conjoin a righteous heart and a happy life. This time of the everyday

ignores the great events that make history. . . . And this time without events
does not get narrated. It is spoken of in proverbs. . . . And yet, it is by way of
the everyday that wisdom brings to light the immemorial, that is, what, as age-
less, has "always existed."

However, in conjoining the everyday with the timeless and immemorial,
biblical wisdom literature begins to shift from its proverbial form of discourse. It does so first by means of a "hypostasis" (found particularly in
Proverbs 8:22–32): the personification or reification of Wisdom. "At this
stage, the immemorial is not just what wisdom says but Wisdom itself
when it speaks."

Eventually, Ricoeur discovers a wisdom agenda operating also in biblical
narrative: "The immemorial time of wisdom . . . reinforces the tendency
of the traditional narratives to become archetypal . . . to the point that
some exegetes have considered these narratives . . . as fragments of a narrativized wisdom or as narratives with a sapiential tone, which amounts to
the same thing." Remarkably, this formulation achieves an inversion of the
'conventional wisdom' which subordinates wisdom either to textualist or to
scientia interests. An alternative view discovers in the archetypal power of
narrative "the spirit of wisdom at the very heart of the narratives." That formulation suggests a *modus vivendi* for encompassing textualist and *scientia* approaches within a wisdom imperative and, therein, attaining "the deep level
where the narrative and the non-narrative interweave and exchange their
respective powers of temporalization." Paul Ricoeur, "Temps biblique,"
Archivio di Filosofia 53 (1985), 29–35. Unpublished English translation by
David Pellauer.

An example of such a "narrativized wisdom" that encompasses textual
and scientific dimensions is the proverbial expression uttered by the physi-
cist Robert Oppenheimer upon viewing the success of his labors, the first
atomic bomb explosion: "I am become death, the destroyer of worlds."
The phrase, lifted from India's epic text, the *Mahabarata,* is freighted with
that narrative and its mythic context, while it also conveys all the horror of
modern science and technology as a series of Frankenstein creations, com-
pletely apart from its original "culture text" (Schreiter) and in resonance
with (variations on) Western culture texts. Would not most students and
their instructors be mutually engaged by such a narrative framing of the
physical sciences and technological development, and therein experience
wisdom "after teaching"?

Rebellious Ethics and Albert Speer

Jack L. Sammons, Jr.

Every task, however simple, sets the soul who does it free.
—*Henry Van Dyke* (Episcopal Hymnal #586)

According to the familiar story, Albert Speer failed to avoid complicity in the Nazi evil surrounding him by not rebelling against his role as Hitler's architect. We teach, preach, and practice professional ethics in this country by holding on to such stories about the morally corrupting effects of our professional roles and the concomitant need to rebel against them. As ethical people, we say, we must stand apart from our professional roles in personal moral judgment of them, in order to avoid becoming an Albert Speer. This is the dominant paradigm for the ethics of our professions. I call this paradigm rebellious ethics, and I want to challenge it by offering a truer telling of the life of Albert Speer and then examining an implication of this truer telling for professional ethics.[1]

The Pure Technician and a Need to Rebel

The paradigmatic version of Speer's story started, oddly enough, when members of the British press recognized that Speer was very much like what most British professionals wanted to be: superbly educated, intelligent, prosperous, powerful, and well bred from good professional

123

stock. He was an effective professional—even an insightful and perceptive one.[2] What the British press saw in Speer in the 1940s, we still see in him today. The traits he displayed as an architect and, later, as Minister of Armaments, are the traits we continue to admire in our professionals.

Because Speer is so much like the professionals we admire, we feel a need to explain his moral failure, and to do so in a way different from our explanations of the moral failure of a Himmler or a Goering or a thousand other petty criminals. By being so like us and yet such a conspicuous moral failure, the story of Speer drives us to define professional ethics in reaction to him. We want professional ethics to be able to separate us from this Speer as easily as we can separate ourselves from a Himmler or a Goering.

The seminal piece for this ethical separation from Speer was written by an English journalist for the British newspaper *The Observer* on April 9, 1944.

> Speer is, in a sense, more important for Germany today than Hitler, Himmler, Goering, Goebbels, or the generals. They all have, in a way, become the mere auxiliaries of the man who actually directs the giant power machine—charged with drawing from it the maximum effort under maximum strain. . . . In him is the very epitome of the "managerial revolution." Speer is not one of the flamboyant and picturesque Nazis. Whether he has any other than conventional political opinions at all is unknown. He might have joined any other political party which gave him a job and a career. He is very much the successful average man, well dressed, civil, noncorrupt, very middle-class in his style of life, with a wife and six children. Much less than any of the other German leaders does he stand for anything particularly German or particularly Nazi. He rather symbolizes a type which is becoming increasingly important in all belligerent countries: the pure technician, the classless bright young man without background, with no other original aim than to make his way in the world and no other means than his technical and managerial ability. . . . This is their age; the Hitlers and Himmlers we may get rid of, but the Speers, whatever happens to this particular special man, will long be with us.

After this article, Speer is no longer Hitler's architect; he is the Pure Technician. But this character is poorly named. The Pure Technician is not a product of technology, although technology may increase his number.[3] His title has much more to do with accountability. The Pure Technician is the expert who is not accountable beyond his area of expertise.[4] His technique, he claims, is morally neutral and he asks to be judged only by whether his means are the most efficient ones toward whatever end is given to him.[5]

By thus characterizing Speer as the Pure Technician we provide a way to separate ourselves from him. We also make clear our motivation for doing so because the Pure Technician is the personification of the moral disease awaiting us if we continue to be like him—that is, if we continue to be wholly captured by our professional roles. Speer the Pure Technician, we know, never reflected beyond what his role as Hitler's architect required of him until it was far too late for a life well lived (if not for his soul), and by not doing so he failed repeatedly to see as people those affected by his acts. Because Speer is so much like us, however, our faith in who we are tells us that Speer the person, as opposed to Speer the professional architect, would have seen as people those affected by his acts if only he had reflected *as a person*. This, however, the Pure Technician cannot do because the Pure Technician always wears the moral blinders of his role. Thus, Speer's moral vision was so impaired by being the Pure Technician that he could not, in a phrase Hauerwas and Burrell use to describe Speer in their perceptive article about him, ". . . spell out [this ethical] feature of his engagement with the world."[6] So Speer, this story tells us, was far too integrated in his role as architect and not well enough integrated in himself for a successful ethical life.[7] If we are to separate ourselves from Speer, then, we must avoid this degree of role integration.

Speer accepted this story about himself in a poignant autobiography he labored over for twenty years in Spandau during his imprisonment after the Nuremberg Trials and finished soon after his release. He was, he said, "above all an architect"[8] who came to think that being Hitler's architect was a sufficient description of a way of life. Because he did, he said, he shut his eyes to the horror around him.[9] So lost in this role was he that he saw no grounds outside the system—a system that was Hitler—where he could take his moral stand.[10] Meditatively, the imprisoned Speer expanded upon his story:

> The nightmare shared by many people. . . that some day the nations of the world may be dominated by technology—that nightmare was very nearly made a reality under Hitler's authoritarian system. Every country in the world today faces the danger of being terrorized by technology, but in a modern dictatorship this seems to me to be unavoidable. Therefore, the more technological the world becomes, the more essential will be the demands for *individual freedom and the self awareness of the individual human being as a counterpoise to technology.*[11]

This, then, is how we are to separate ourselves from Speer. We will not be like him if we take our professions much less seriously than he did and ourselves much more seriously, but to do this, we must do what Speer did not: We must consciously maintain a personal and psychological detachment from our professional roles. By doing so, we free ourselves for the personal reflection so plainly missing from Speer's life. For it is in our personal detachment from role that we find the moral distance needed for spelling out our full engagement with the world.

But our roles are very imposing, and preserving our personal moral freedom from them is an extremely difficult moral task. If we want to avoid the morally corrupting forces of professional role Speer suffered, we must consciously adopt and steadfastly maintain the personal and psychological stance of the *moral rebel* against our professions. Thus, the answer professional ethics gives to the challenge presented by Speer's life, and the paradigm in which professional ethics works, is for professional ethics to be rebellious.

There is a long and complex history behind the development of the moral psychology of the rebel—it is, perhaps, a reflection of art's much earlier association with self-projection and the singular voice[12]—but the extreme degree of its current manifestation in professional ethics (the extent, that is, to which Speer the Pure Technician haunts us) is surely a recent phenomenon. Over the past one hundred and twenty years, the ethics of the legal profession, for example, have evolved quickly from the professional to the personal, from an internal source for ethical judgments to a purely external source for conduct.[13]

Despite the recentness of its current domination, however, this rebellious stance has now become so ingrained in our ethical thinking about professional roles that to challenge it is to risk great misunderstanding, if not moral condemnation. But this risk we must take, because there is a truer telling of the story of Speer's moral failure, one which challenges the rebellious ethics paradigm. This telling of his life teaches us that professionals should be good at what they do—better than Speer was. It says that Speer's moral failure was *as an architect*[14] and that it is in greater, not lesser, integration with his role that Speer could have had the moral resources—the distance, the vision, and the courage—he needed to see that he, too, released the gas and fired the ovens. This truer telling condemns Speer more strongly than the story of Speer the Pure Technician because it asks about moral resources available to Speer in the story of the architect he professed to live by. It also condemns him by being more consistent with his autobiography than his own conclusions were. From this, we can see that Speer's self-deception—for this is how Hauerwas and Burrell describe his being dominated by his role[15]—continued in Spandau on Speer's own terms; that is, on terms he could have accepted as Hitler's architect. This version of Speer's life condemns us, too, by revealing how much like Hitler's architect we continue to be, and how we cannot separate ourselves from him by a facile rebellion against our professional roles. It says we are failing, as Speer failed, because we do not take our professions seriously enough.

The Failed Architect

The familiar story of Speer is right when it says that Speer came to rely on his role as an architect as a sufficient morality. (Later, as I shall describe, he discovered that his morality was also based on a story about the German people, a story he seldom understood as an architect although, ironically, this story was part of his understanding of good architecture.) There were other moralities available to the young Speer, but Speer rejected the moralities of his parents, as did so many young Germans of the time, along with much of his past,[16] and the older Speer never reconciled himself to them or to the moral stories in which his family had lived for generations. He did not understand himself as being in these stories or "see their relevance to the chaos around him."[17] Nor could the older Speer find a relevant morality as a husband or as a father sufficient to challenge his self-deceptions as Hitler's architect. A different person, perhaps, could have judged his life as a Nazi with an understanding of himself as a good husband or as a good father, but Speer needed more of a community for his moral reflections (as I believe most Germans did) than the family could provide. It would have been extremely difficult for Speer to understand the relationship between the practical and the spiritual—as he so needed to do to see his situation truthfully—in the community of his family. But it should have been far easier for him to do so in the community of the practical and the spiritual that good architecture can be. And this was the community in which Speer located himself. This is what he meant when he said he was "above all an architect."

While the familiar story is right about Speer's reliance on role as a sufficient morality, the implication of this reliance should not be the one rebellious ethics draws, that is, that this reliance limited Speer's moral reflections. For to deny to Speer a deep engagement with architecture, to ask him to take his profession less seriously, would be to deny him the only morality he had that could place him outside Hitler's system for reflection and thus provide him with something moral to proclaim from that external stance. We can see that this is true by looking at his life as an architect more closely.

The Moral Lessons of Architecture

Until very near the end of the war, Speer's only moments of moral insight into the truth of his situation as Hitler's architect—the only times he came close to spelling out his full engagement with the world—were those of architectural insights.[18] As an architect, Speer began to see in Hitler's obsession with huge dimensions,[19] his "violation of the human scale,"[20] his lack of proportion, his lack of concern for the social dimension of architecture,[21] his use of architecture as only an expression of his strength, and the pomposity and decadence of his style, a dictator bent on world domination for the sole purpose of his own glorification—a megalomaniacal tyrant, full of hubris and entirely lacking in compassion and balance. Architecture also revealed to Speer the horrifying contradictions in Hitler's life, contradictions that later gave Speer the strength to oppose him.

What architecture offered Speer, however, was more than just a different perception of the person to whom he had turned over his life. Architecture also began to tell Speer who *he* had become as Hitler's architect. As with many of his architectural insights into reality, this lesson came first to Speer while he was on an art tour gathering ideas for his designs. Describing the Escorial, a complex comparable to Hitler's Fuhrer Palace in its proportions, he said:

> What a contrast with Hitler's architectural ideas: in the one case, remarkable conciseness and clarity, magnificent interior rooms, their form perfectly controlled; in the other case, pomp and disproportionate ostentation.[22]

Speer saw this contrast as expressing an impulse underlying the Escorial "quite different and far more spiritual," he said, than the impulse underlying his own work. Following this visit, he had an epiphany: "In hours of solitary contemplation it began to dawn on me for the first time that my recent architectural ideals were on the wrong track."[23]

Thus architecture offered Speer a truer perspective on Hitler and on himself, for the moral vision this German and this Nazi needed to criticize the acts of the popular hero who ruled his country, and to understand himself, could come best from the only separate community available to him in which the virtues could still be defined and understood. It was in a practice in which the practical and the spiritual could be combined, as they are when architecture is good, that he could see the limitations of Hitler's insistence upon the primacy of the practical. (As Hitler once stated: "For there can be only one single rule, and this rule, put succinctly, is: That is correct which is useful in itself."[24])

By being an architect, Speer could continue an imaginary conversation within a community of architects extending over time (and a conversation with his mentor, a person I will describe later). This public-private conversation requires a more explicit spelling out of engagements; it requires more explanations than the private conversation of rebellious ethics—the conversation of the "two-in-one" in Hannah Arendt's phrase. This architectural conversation continues eternally as a dialogue that reveals the teleology of architecture. It continues because the good architect knows it would be the death of architecture, as others have said it would be the death of religion, to cling to the last revelation.

The public-private conversation of architecture differs sharply from what remained of true public conversations in Hitler's system. As told by Speer:

> The ordinary party member was being taught that grand policy was much too complex for him to judge it. Consequently, one felt one was being represented, never called upon to take personal responsibility. The whole structure of the system was aimed at preventing conflicts of conscience from even arising. The result was the total sterility of all conversations and discussions among these like-minded persons. It was boring for people to confirm one another in their uniform opinions. . . . What eventually developed was a society of totally isolated individuals.[25]

The public-private conversation Speer could have as an architect could place him in a community outside this "society of totally isolated individuals" in which he could only see himself. By doing so, it could give him a moral distance from Hitler, and the skills he needed to spell out his full engagement with the world. At its best, architecture could have been for Speer the "good companion" that David Kolb claims it can be:

> So architecture makes a good companion. Architects have grappled in detail with problems of rootedness and continuity. The surrounding environment cannot be wished away; the ways people live cannot be arbitrarily

changed; all this must be taken into account, which is not to say it must be passively accepted. We can learn from the discipline and facticity of architecture not to be taken in by extreme positions that claim for us a freedom either wider or more narrow than the freedom we have. The difficulties of creating good architecture can illuminate our tasks in building cultures and worlds together amid the products of our past.[26]

As Speer himself knew, for example, it was only through his preliminary architectural studies—and through none other—that he had acquired the ability to examine various points of view with a lack of conscious bias.[27]

Speer's Failure to Learn

Writing in Spandau, however, Speer failed to understand the morality that architecture could have been for him. Instead, he accepted the way others had characterized him:

I so rarely—in fact almost never—found the time to reflect about myself or my own activities, that I never gave my own existence a thought. Today, in retrospect, I often have the feeling that something swooped me up off the ground at the time, wrenched me from all my roots, and beamed a host of alien forces upon me. In retrospect, what perhaps troubled me most is that my occasional spells of uneasiness during this period were concerned mainly with the direction I was taking as an architect, with my growing estrangement from [my mentor's] doctrine.[28]

It was not until after he left Spandau that the now pensive Speer, looking back at his work, could see more clearly what had been the obvious lessons of architecture. The Nazi style, he saw now, was "decadent baroque, comparable to the style that accompanied the decline of the Roman Empire. . . ," and "neoclassicism. . . multiplied, altered, exaggerated, and sometimes distorted to the point of ludicrousness."

Speer's failure to learn the moral lessons of architecture, and, accordingly, his failure as an architect, are symbolized in the gilded eagle he designed for the great domed hall that was to be the architectural center of Hitler's power. For the post-Spandau Speer, this eagle became the

symbol of what architecture could have taught him about Hitler, but did
not, and of the person he could have been, but was not:

> Had I been able to think the matter out consistently, I ought to have argued
> further that my designs for Hitler were following the pattern of the Late Em-
> pire and forecasting the end of the regime; that, therefore, Hitler's downfall
> could be deduced from these very designs. But this [decadence] was hidden
> from me at the time. And not only the style but the excessive size of these
> buildings plainly revealed Hitler's intention. One day in the early summer of
> 1939, he pointed to the German eagle with the swastika in its claws which
> was to crown the dome nine hundred fifty-seven feet in the air. "That has to
> be changed. Instead of the swastika, the eagle is to be perched above the
> globe." There are photos of the models in which this revision is plainly to be
> seen. A few months later the Second World War began.[29]

Surveying his life, he knew now what he did not know then:

> "What is more, by my abilities and my energies I had prolonged that war by
> many months. I had assented to having the globe of the world crown that
> domed hall which was to be the symbol of the new Berlin."[30]

After Spandau, Speer could also see what being Hitler's architect had
done to him as an architect:

> And I moved with [his tendency towards pomposity]. For my designs of
> this period owed less and less to what I regarded as "my style." This es-
> trangement from my beginnings was revealed in other ways beside the
> wildly excessive size of my buildings. They had become pure "art of deca-
> dence." Wealth, the inexhaustible funds at my disposal, but also Hitler's
> party ideology, had led me along the path to a style which drew its inspira-
> tion rather from the show palaces of Oriental despots.[31]

Thus Speer knew he had turned his back on reality, something he knew
a good architect must never do in his work.[32] But, as he also understood,
the eyes he had used as an architect were not his own: he saw all his
buildings with Hitler's political eyes. Because he did, Speer, too, came
to be ruled by the practical and, as a result, "on the plane of feeling only

sentimentality emerged. . . ."[33] This was a utility that swept aside his architectural sense. He did not just turn his back on reality; he brushed it away. "In the euphoria of history-making activity, unpleasant facts were ignored; they were no more than obstacles to the achievement of the grand design."[34]

And so Speer failed to learn the moral lessons architecture offered him. But why? In May 1935, when Speer visited Delphi, the model for his work for Hitler, on his first trip abroad, he made a discovery:

> The purity of Greek artistic creativeness was speedily contaminated by the wealth won in the Ionian colonies in Asia. Didn't this prove how sensitive a high artistic consciousness was and how little it took to distort the ideal conception to the point of unrecognizability? I happily played with such theories; it never occurred to me that my own works might be subject to these same laws.[35]

But why did it not occur to him? Why had he come to see the world with his client's eyes and not his own architecturally trained ones? We can account for this failure, as we always should in the case of professions, by looking for corruption. When we do, we see Speer as something far different from Speer the Pure Technician, and we see something far different from a Speer who is "above all" an architect. We see, instead, Speer the Failed Architect.

The Corruption of a Profession

Speer failed architecture by corrupting his craft in a very common way. It is the old story of hubris, as Davidson calls it in his discerning foreward to Speer's autobiography.[36] As an architect, Speer sought pride and position and the opportunity to create on a heroic scale. In doing so, he defined success as an architect only in terms of the external goods it could provide, the ones that have little to do with the craft itself.[37] As Speer said: "After years of frustrated efforts I was wild to accomplish things—and twenty-eight years old. For the commission to do a great building, I would have sold my soul like Faust." The soul he offered to his

Mephistopheles was not just the one he was referring to; he offered his architectural soul as well. By seeking only the external goods of his profession, Speer eventually denied himself the moral distance and the moral direction it could provide.[38]

Speer's corruption of architecture began in his break with his architectural mentor, Professor Heinrich Tessenow,[39] a man whose work Speer described as "a champion of the spirit of simple craftsmanship in architecture and belief in architectonic expressiveness by severely delimited means. 'A minimum of pomp is the decisive factor.'"[40]

Tessenow taught the young Speer: "Style comes from the people. It is our nature to love our native land. There can be no true culture that is international. True culture comes only from the maternal womb of a nation." Speer and other students saw parallels between Tessenow's doctrine and the ideology of the National Socialists, but Tessenow did not, and he remained firmly opposed to Hitler. Despite his mentor's opposition, however, Speer, influenced by his National Socialists colleagues, joined the Party.

A few years later, when Speer showed Tessenow drawings he had done for an enthusiastic Hitler, Tessenow responded: "Do you think you have created something? It's showy, that's all."[41] Tessenow must have known that Hitler's cultural expressionism was mere ostentation, vanity, and pride and not a truthful reflection of the people at all. This was a style of architecture that could not spell out the uniqueness of the German people's engagement with the world, which is what Tessenow thought architecture should be doing. It was, instead, a mirrored reflection of Hitler, used as a cheap trick to manipulate those it claimed to represent. But the young Speer missed this lesson from his mentor. Grand praise from the Fuhrer more than compensated for his mentor's lack of respect for his work. By this move, Speer came to see his success as an architect as indistinguishable from recognition by the State and this, then, in the dictatorship that was Germany, reduced to recognition by Hitler alone. Speer became an architect obsessed with a single, immensely powerful and violent client whose pleasure defined success for him. Necessarily, as he sought self-respect as an architect from Hitler's praise, he rejected his craft.

For Hitler to serve well in its place, Speer needed desperately to admire this man who affirmed his being.[42]

> Only a few months before I had been carried away by the prospect of drafting and executing buildings. Now I was completely under Hitler's spell, unreservedly and unthinkingly held by him. I was ready to follow him anywhere. Yet his ostensible interest in me was only to launch me on a glorious career as an architect.[43]

This Speer mimics the infamous hired gun of legal ethics defining success by doing well whatever the client wants. As is true for the hired gun, however, Speer was not dominated by his client on architectural matters.[44] As he said: "If the architect's ideas ran counter to his own, Hitler was not stubborn: 'Yes, you're right, that's better.' The result was that I too was left with the feeling of creative independence."[45] But also as is true for the hired gun, Speer tried to separate his architectural function from all others and, thus, his understanding of architectural matters—the grounds on which he was free to think for himself were very limited. "I am only concerned with what is legal," the hired gun says, "the rest is none of my business." And Speer echoes:

> I felt myself to be Hitler's architect. Political events did not concern me. My job was merely to provide impressive backdrops for such events. And this view was reinforced daily, for Hitler consulted me almost exclusively on architectural questions. . . . I felt that there was no need for me to take any political position at all. Nazi education, furthermore, aimed at separatist thinking; I was expected to confine myself to the job of building. The grotesque extent to which I clung to this illusion is indicated by a memorandum of mine to Hitler as late as 1944: "The task I have to fulfill is an unpolitical one. I have felt at ease in my work only so long as my person and my work were evaluated solely by the standard of practical accomplishments."[46]

Within the limited range in which he understood his work, Speer thought he retained his judgment. But it was not judgment he retained; it was only expertise. For Speer's problem was not that he could not judge what his client was doing, it was that he did not see such judgments as within his role. Speer thought that architecture could be separated from all else; he thought that the practical and the spiritual could be held apart, as he tried to hold politics apart from "practical accomplishments."[47] But the world cannot be dissevered this way and neither can architecture, as Speer knew when he later looked upon the vast gilded eagle with its claws over the globe.[48]

Speer's drive to get ahead and what became of it—his corruption of his profession by seeking only external goods, in MacIntyre's now classic terms—is a very common form of corruption. It was a corruption of architecture by Speer as it would be a corruption of law, of medicine, of engineering, of business, of art, or of religion. This commonplace corruption best explains Speer's failure to reflect and not some lack of personal moral distance from his profession. The moral distance Speer needed for reflection was there to be found within the profession itself. The truth for Speer, something that sounds ironic only from the perspective of rebellious ethics, is that it was in further integration with architecture that he could have seen his responsibility for the world around him.

This truer story of Albert Speer is closer to home for us than the story of Speer the Pure Technician. Speer the Failed Architect draws us into his story in a way that rebellious ethics cannot. It says: We cannot escape the ghost of Speer by not taking our jobs so seriously. We can do so only by taking them more seriously in the right way.[49]

Near the end of the war, Speer left his position as Hitler's architect to become Minister of Armaments. There was no discontinuity in this for him because he could achieve the external goods he sought as an architect just as well as a bureaucrat. By understanding success as tied to Hitler's approval, he was trying to live, as some other professionals do, by the prestige and power of his client rather than by the excellence of his craft. Accordingly, architecture itself became irrelevant and only Hitler's approval ultimately mattered. Speer, however, thought of his position as Minister of Armaments as a temporary departure from architecture. He continued to see himself as an architect because, as he put it, "I saw the possibility of winning a reputation, and even fame, as Hitler's architect whereas whatever even a prominent minister could accomplish would necessarily be absorbed in Hitler's glory." At this stage of his life, Speer could see no reason for being an architect other than the external goods it could provide.[50]

Ironically, it was as a bureaucrat, the archetypical role for the Pure Technicians we fear, that Speer turned upon Hitler.[51] He did so for reasons that return us by an interesting route to his former mentor, Professor Tessenow. Speer began his separation from Hitler when he heard Hitler discussing the devastation of Warsaw. He saw Hitler "wantonly and without cause annihilating the city which he himself had called the most beautiful in Europe . . . . Within a few days," Speer goes on, "some of the contradictions in Hitler's nature had been revealed to me, although at the time I certainly did not perceive them in anything like their full intensity."[52]

From this point on, Speer turned steadily against Hitler. Later, he thought the morality he relied upon to support his opposition was a morality he learned from Hitler—one taken almost directly from the text of *Mein Kampf,* a text Speer had paid little attention to before. From *Mein Kampf* and from his colleagues, Speer began to understand the story in which he lived as one about the German people. He saw that the essential element of all he had done was that he was doing it for them. This element, this one remaining piece of integrity that made any sense of Speer's life at all, Hitler violated when he turned on the German people as the world began to corner him. Finally Speer was learning the lesson his mentor had offered so many years before: the difference between Tessenow's architectural need to spell out truthfully the German culture and the German people, and Hitler's use of the ideas of a culture and a people for personal political power. At the end of the war, we can see as Speer could not an immanent integrity in what could have been his life as an architect and how this would have shaped him and saved him from himself.[53]

I am tempted to stop here. If I have told this story well, it makes my point, and if I have not, I probably will only make it worse with further explication. But if Suzi Gablik is right (and I believe she is) when she describes in *Has Modernism Failed,*[54] what happened to art when it adopted the artistic equivalent of rebellious ethics—how the practice of art became corrupted as artist sought only external success and security—and if art is our miner's canary, then what I have described as Speer's corruption of architecture may be what lies just ahead for all professions (if it has not yet arrived) as we continue within the paradigm of rebellious ethics. Rebellious ethics, in its effort to separate us from Speer, seems to leave us as morally exposed as Speer became. Are we not as obsessed with pride and position—or their more timid relative, security—as the young Speer was in rejecting his craft? Now I must wonder why this is so. Why does rebellious ethics fail us? The answer to this is, of course, a large task, too large for one article, but one component of the answer is that rebellious ethics cannot provide a conception of the self that rebels adequate to protect us from becoming as self-deceived as Albert Speer.

To return to our starting place, according to rebellious ethics, Speer the person, unlike Speer the Pure Technician, would have seen the horror around him. Rebellious ethics proclaims this because Speer is so much like us and we have faith in who we are. Speer needs to take his profession less seriously—far less seriously—and himself far more seriously. He performs this difficult moral task by constantly rebelling against his role as an architect. But who is this self that rebels? Who is this self that we must take so seriously? And who is this self that is so like us that we trust it?

The Roleless Person

One answer is that this self is the authentic self of existentialist thought. To reflect from the broadest, and therefore the least limiting, perspective possible, the authentic self must not identify itself with any role. This moral rebel could not be Speer the German, nor Speer the Christian, nor Speer the citizen, nor Speer the father or husband, nor Speer as *a* Speer nor even Speer as Speer, because these are just other blinding roles, equally relativistic, reflection-limiting choices of a way of life— especially so, for some of them, in Nazi Germany. The moral rebel of rebellious ethics whose reflections we trust is Speer the Roleless Person. This, then, is one possible "self" rebellious ethics tells us to become for our reflections upon our professional roles if we are to avoid becoming Speer the Pure Technician.[55]

If we have learned anything at all from postmodern philosophy, however, it is that our reflections always come from a particular perspective and both imply and need a teleology.[56] Because this way of identifying the moral rebel does not examine the perspective or the teleology, it becomes not a faith in the moral rebel, but a faith in reflection alone. It is reflection, then, and not ourselves, that we must take more seriously. This faith in reflection is what Stanley Fish has called the "anti-foundationalist theory hope," and it is a bad faith because it leaves us as vulnerable to self-deception as Speer was.[57]

Hauerwas and Burrell, as I have said, tell us that the story of Speer's life is a story of self-deception,[58] a self-deception that

> . . . was correlative to his identity as he clung to the story of being Hitler's apolitical architect. . . . He had no effective way to step back from himself, no place to stand. His self-deception began when he assumed that "being above all an architect" was a story sufficient to constitute his self. He had to experience the solitude of prison to realize that becoming a human being requires stories and images a good deal richer than professional ones, if we are to be equipped to deal with the powers of the world.[59]

Hauerwas and Burrell imply that we cannot remove this risk of self-deception with a belief in reflection alone because, without a complete and truthful account of the moral rebel against which self-deception can be measured and understood, we cannot know if we are self-deceived.[60] Thus, reduced as we are by rebellious ethics, we are easy prey for the twin demons of pride and position, especially, and ironically, when they are offered by a powerful and charismatic leader for whom the world is a simple place. So, with terrible irony, these efforts within the paradigm of rebellious ethics to separate ourselves from Speer the Pure Technician leave us open to the same moral failure he suffered.

Master Stories

Rebellious ethics needs not, however, find its perspective for reflection in the Roleless Person. Another answer rebellious ethics can give to the question of this self we are to take more seriously is the answer Hauerwas and Burrell gave in the quotation above when they said: "[Speer] had to experience the solitude of prison to realize that becoming a human being requires stories and images a good deal richer than professional ones, if we are to be equipped to deal with the powers of the world." This answer does not suffer from a bad faith in reflection alone and, because it does not, it is willing to abandon the claim that we must reflect from the broadest perspective possible. This answer locates the self we must take more seriously in stories and images "a good deal richer than professional ones." Instead of asking Speer to be a good person we should ask that he be a good Christian, for example. Stories such as this one, Hauerwas and Burrell tell us, are more richly connected, and, because they are, permit us to spell out our full engagement with the world more truthfully.

There is much more sophistication in this version of rebellious ethics, but it is still rebellious ethics. Hauerwas and Burrell, who would be the first to find reflection alone, and the Roleless Person, thoroughly inadequate moral groundings, complain of Speer's failure to live by a "master story"[61] capable of providing him with the moral skills he needed. It is only within a "master story" that reflection has the power to recognize alternatives. The power, that is, to criticize and change.[62]

But even for Hauerwas and Burrell, we still distance ourselves from Speer by not taking our jobs so seriously. When we do, Speer the Failed Architect awaits us. For what Hauerwas and Burrell miss is that Speer's self-deception ran deeper than his belief "that 'being above all an architect' was a story sufficient to constitute his self."[63] Speer did not live by this belief. He did not, as they describe it, turn to his profession, for a "story [with which] to articulate the engagements he would be called upon to undertake."[64] He turned away from the story his profession offered him and turned, instead, toward himself in an act of corruption of his profession. When Speer says, as he often does in his autobiography, that he was "above all an architect," he was only deceiving himself further. He was above all Albert Speer.[65]

Hauerwas and Burrell's Speer is still Speer the Pure Technician. It is still his role as architect that another Speer within an overarching narrative must rebel against. This rebellion, it is true, is now grounded in a self located within the overarching narrative, and, therefore, it has a perspective and a teleology for its reflections. There is no doubt that such a Speer could criticize and change. But we cannot stop with this solution. We have to ask: What would Hauerwas and Burrell say to the Speer who was Hitler's architect *as he was* as Hitler's architect? Would their advice to live by a richer story be as powerful for him as it is for us looking back on his life? How would they have counseled him? We must ask these questions and ask them in this way, for this is the way we ask moral questions of ourselves. We are not looking back over our lives from outside our roles or our stories, but from within them.[66]

Would it be possible for Hauerwas and Burrell to counsel the Nazi Speer about his need to find an overarching narrative for his life? Would they be reduced to seeking to impose upon him an overarching narrative in which they have found meaning? Would they counsel Speer by their own actions—actions they are moved to by their narrative? (I am sure they would.) But, if they did, would the Nazi Speer be capable of learning this moral lesson from them? Given Speer's description of his rejection of his past, of the inadequacies of his early education for critical thinking, of Hitler's techniques for isolating and compartmentalizing, of the lack of criticism around him, of his own hubris, and so forth, and given Hitler's promise to Speer that he would design the cities of a new empire, it would have been pointless to tell Speer that he should be living by a richer story.[67] Speer himself says as much: "In spite of all our dissensions [the thought to resign my post in order to put an end to my contribution to Hitler's regime] did not come to me then and in a similar situation probably would not come to me today."[68] Interestingly, Speer's primary reaction to reading *The Observer's* article in 1944 was Faustian pride that he had been singled out for such recognition and a fear that others would be jealous of it.[69]

But there is another way for Hauerwas and Burrell to counsel Speer. They could seek a moral meeting ground with the Nazi Speer within the practice of architecture. In its potential for combining the spiritual and the practical there lies a way—and, perhaps, the only way—for the Nazi Speer to see his life as within a narrative of the sort Hauerwas and Burrell describe. In Hauerwas and Burrell's terms, it was only in architecture that Speer could have found the imaginative and intellectual skills sufficient to overcome those he used to create a web of illusion lending plausibility to his original deceptive policy.[70] This meeting ground, however, would be lost to Hauerwas and Burrell because they join the chorus of rebellious ethics telling Speer: Do not take your profession too seriously. In doing so, they too would have unwillingly moved the Nazi Speer to further separate the spiritual and the practical.[71] And, if we are like Speer, we must be concerned that this move in professional ethics would do the same for us.

Surely, then, what was needed for Speer—and for us—it not a hierarchy of narratives, but the moral ability to see the interconnections between one narrative and another. The truth the church—the one in which Hauerwas and Burrell's overarching narrative lives—brings to architecture is not a truth that overarches. It is a vision and imagination formed by being in that church. It is the moral ability to speak the truth of architecture to it.[72] What is needed, then, is the vision and the imagination to see how the good architect, and the good person and, for Hauerwas and Burrell and for me, the good Christian, can be one and the same.

Church and Craft

Of course, what is behind Hauerwas and Burrell's claim is a desire for the church to stand against the nation by being the nonviolent alternative community to its force and coercion. But the relationship the church needs to have with the nation cannot be the model for its relationship with the arts, crafts, and professions. These the church must claim for itself. In fact, one of the ways for the church to stand against nation, as that term is used by Hauerwas,[73] is for the church to take the arts, crafts, and professions more seriously than they take themselves. And this is what I would ask the church to do in Speer's case. For it is only through the church that we can understand Speer's life and work as the lie to God that it was. We do so by first understanding architecture as a spiritual task (and by understanding some spiritual tasks as architecture). When we do this we take architecture more seriously than architecture takes itself. We would all feel more comfortable about this if we said "take architecture more seriously as a theological matter." But the point of the church of history should be to deny that there is a difference between these statements. If this is true, why would we want to separate ourselves from the spiritual tasks of our work as rebellious ethics asks us to do?

Said differently, it is one thing to say (as Hauerwas does) that the church's social mission is first to be the church because the church is to be an alternative community to those of power. To speak truth to power the church must first know truth, Hauerwas teaches; but, he goes on, the truth the church can know and speak is not something that can be separated from the task of being the church because the truth is a matter of continuing vision and imagination. This is what it means for the church not to *have* an ethic, but to *be* one. In this context, we can readily understand the church's claims of being an alternative community and how this alternative community must stand against those who claim to offer control over our lives in ways that do not recognize that life itself is a gift.

It is quite another thing, however, to say that the church is also an alternative community to our communities of craft, art, and profession. In what sense is the church an alternative community here? What is the vision and imagination the church could bring, not to our lives, but to our work? I think the task here is different. The relationship of the church to craft, art, and profession must be softer than any of our spatial descriptions about narratives imply (as is perfectly clear in the relationship between the church and music). The church is not over (or under, against, reformative of, subordinately reciprocated to) these activities. This description misses the necessary interconnection—necessary, that is, if the church is to be in the world, but not of it, and if our lives are to be as theologically lived as the church requires.

If the alternative that the church is is one of *continuing* vision and imagination—if it is not fixed—then the church should not subordinate alternatives to itself, as implied by a claim of an overarching narrative. To subordinate other narratives eliminates alternative perspectives and, with them, part of the vision and imagination the church could be. This is counterproductive for a church that is there to be an alternative community, and it means that we come to need an alternative to the alternative provided by the church. (This, it seems to me, is why Hauerwasians—and

I gladly include myself among their number—are so seldom pleased with what most churches do.) For to provide alternatives, the church must come to know fully the world that the church provides the alternative to, and this means knowing the many and different ways in which the world can be viewed. Other ways of doing this makes the church define itself in reaction to a view of the world that the church posits as *the* view of the world (and then calls it nation or culture or some equally all-encompassing word). In doing so, the church separates itself from the world in a way that can only harm both the church and the world.[74]

Conclusion

We can let Speer teach us to rebel against all roles, or we can, with Hauerwas and Burrell, bewail Speer's failure, and our own, to live by richer stories such as those of the church. The Roleless Person of rebellious ethics tells us to be *nothing* too seriously, for in commitment comes a limitation on the perspective for our reflections and it is our reflections that ground our morality. Hauerwas and Burrell say be something richer than that which our professional roles can provide.[75] But we cannot ask the Nazi Speer to do either without rewriting his biography. And we cannot do either without distancing ourselves from Speer and from our own professional lives in ways that only disservice our efforts to understand his moral failure and, by understanding his, to understand our own. We are like Speer as we are now. In our obsessions with pride, position, and security, in our hubris, we are seeing our world through the eyes of our masters—those who can provide these goods for us—and not through our own. The method we have chosen for separating ourselves from Speer, rebellious ethics, ironically, only moves us closer to him.

My thanks to Robert Audi, Joe Allegretti, Ted Blumoff, Joe Claxton, Tom Eisele, Howard Lesnick, Dave Oedel, Richard Vance, and Sidney Watson for comments, to J. Shand Watson for an ongoing conversation on similar topics, and a very special thanks to Stanley Hauerwas, Michael Goldberg, and Tom Shaffer for their comments and encouragement. As usual, thanks also to Tedham Porterhouse for inspiration. With friends like these, I should have been able to get this right and none of them is to be blamed for my failure to do so.

NOTES

1. The term "paradigm" is too weak for what I want to describe if it does not remind the reader of the mythic foundations of our ethics. The paradigm of rebellious ethics may be grounded in the Faust myth with the professions in the role of Mephistopheles or Lucifer depending upon the version of the myth. If this is true, then this article is about competing interpretations of this myth for our times.

2. He saw, for example, as Minister of Armaments, the need to create an improvisational style for organizations if the Germans were to match the creativity of the allies. He knew enough about German authoritarianism to understand its proclivity toward complex organizational structures that reduce efficiency by searching too hard for it. Albert Speer, *Inside the Third Reich* (New York: Avon Books, 1970), 212–13.

3. Technology made falling prey to role domination an easier matter than it had been before by creating new roles removed from the traditions of crafts and serving narrower functions at a greater distance from those served by the role.

4. "[H]e treats ends as given, as outside his scope; his concern is with technique. . . . " Alasdair MacIntyre, *After Virtue,* (Notre Dame: University of Notre Dame Press, 1984), 30. MacIntyre is describing the character "The Manager."

5. MacIntyre traces this claim of moral neutrality to the fact/value distinction. This distinction serves an ideology of efficiency justifying the character of the Manager. *After Virtue,* 74–108. We cannot simply abandon the character of the Manager because he is essential to the predictability of human affairs needed to complete his own justification. What we must do—and here I anticipate part of the argument—is to define a self in reaction to The Manager in which the responsibility for morality resides. *Id* at 31–35. Defining this self is a problem for rebellious ethics. See *infra* n. 59–81.

6. Stanley Hauerwas and David Burrell, "Self-Deception and Autobiography: Reflections on Speer's *Inside the Third Reich,* " in Hauerwas, *Truthfulness and Tragedy* (Notre Dame: University of Notre Dame Press, 1977) 83–84.

7. This criticism makes Speer's selection of the following quotation from Karl Barth to begin his autobiography interesting:

> Every autobiography is a dubious enterprise. For the underlying assumption is that a chair exists in which a man can sit down to contemplate his own life, to compare its phrases, to survey its development, and to penetrate its meaning.

> Every man can and surely ought to take stock of himself. But he cannot survey
> himself even in the present moment, any more than in the whole of his past.

8. Speer, 21.

9. Speer, 376.

10. Speer, 375.

11. Speer, 521. This passage is from Speer's speech at Nuremberg. Emphasis
has been added.

12. The history of the moral rebel may also mesh with the history of science's
independence from society. If so, then we can trace this back to Galileo
and earlier. Science moved toward autonomy to become universal and im-
partial, a move that is similar to the move of rebellious ethics. We may
also find another part of this history in the evolution of term "good"
from its original functional meaning. When "good" left the context of
functions within a polis (such as the good warrior), it had to find a context broader than the polis and it did so by becoming a universal term, that
is, by becoming a term we could apply to any individual without specific
regard for relative context. After this it became possible to wonder if
someone could be a "good person," in contrast with a good lawyer or a
good architect, for example, in a way that was not possible when good was
a functional term. Prior to this, what I am calling roles were definitive of
the self and could not be taken on or thrown off anymore than one's identify could be. See Alasdair MacIntyre, *A Short History of Ethics* (New
York: Collier Books 1966) 35, 84–109. MacIntyre tells us that what I
have called the moral rebel, and he the emotivist self, is the product of a
reaction to "those characters which inhabit and present the dominant social roles" such as the Manager (*After Virtue*, 34). In other words, the
moral rebel exists only as a relationship to the characters by which
modernity structures and understands our social interconnections. Finally, there is also an intimate relationship between the history of the
moral rebel and the liberal privatization of religion.

    Some of these versions of the history of the moral rebel would make his
emergence a rather recent event. But others have seen the role-distance of
the moral rebel as anticipated in Stoic thought and not as a feature distin-
guishing modernity from antiquity. See Charles E. Larmore, *Patterns
of Moral Complexity*, (Cambridge: Cambridge University Press 1987)
chapter 2, n. 7, and chapter 5. In his book, *Sources of the Self: The Making
of Modern Identity* (Cambridge: Harvard Univ. Press, 1989), Professor

Charles Taylor writes of this disengaged self as having its sources in a certain idea of inwardness beginning with Augustine (although it seems to me that the role authority plays in Augustine's conception of understanding makes him blameless for what we may have made of his work).

13. The current standard conception of the role morality of lawyering, for example, says that the degree to which turn-of-the-century lawyers were morally integrated with their role was, and is, a morally risky way of thinking. It is risky because good moral thinking is based upon a foundation of a recognition of others as having certain entitlements by virtue of their being persons and nothing else. This foundation is called common morality by the standard conception and it is not something that has anything to do with being in any role, including the role of lawyer. In fact, the standard conception requires all lawyers to dissociate from their roles to some meaningful degree to stand in moral judgment of the acts the roles require of them. The lawyer cannot abdicate moral responsibility when in her role because moral responsibility is inalienable. What the lawyer must do to remain moral in her role is to hold on to common moral responsibility in a part of her person which always stands outside of the role and in judgment of it—the rebellious part. See David Luban, *Lawyers and Justice: An Ethical Study* (Princeton: Princeton University Press, 1988). It is ironic to describe this as a standard conception of role morality, since those who espouse it do so in an attack on what they call the standard conception of the morality of the practice of law, by which they mean the conception premised upon the dual principles of neutrality and partisanship. But I think it is correct to call this conception of role morality standard. For my generation of lawyers and law professors, this conception found its first expression in Wasserstrom, "Lawyers as Professionals: Some Moral Issues," *Human Rights Quarterly* vol. 5, no. 1, 105 (1975). I think this is the conception of role morality that drives most courses in "Professional Responsibility." There, professors teach students that being a "person" is morally superior to being a lawyer and this is what the standard conception is all about.

This standard conception can become quite sophisticated—I am tempted to say convoluted—in its efforts to work out some balance between role and common morality. It must work out this balance to hold on to its foundational distinction: that is, to keep role morality from collapsing into common morality. David Luban's solution in *Lawyers and Justice* is something he playfully calls the Fourfold Root of Sufficient Reason.

Very simply, it amounts to a careful assessment of the strength of the policy concerns unique to lawyering as applied to a particular situation faced by a lawyer. The product of the Fourfold Root is then balanced against common morality in a straightforward manner. (*Lawyers,* 128–139.) Luban later described this analysis as waffling between consequentialism and deontology. See Luban, "Freedom and Constraint in Legal Ethics: Some Mid-Course Corrections" to *Lawyers and Justice,* 49 *Md. L. Rev.* 424, 429 (1990). He did so in response to a criticism by David Wasserman that a consequentialist balancing would almost always favor common morality. This was true because each individual act of deviation from the role would have only a marginal consequentialist effect on the policy concerns unique to lawyering. See Wasserman, "Should a Good Lawyer Do the Right Thing? David Luban on the Morality of Adversary Representation," 49 *Md. Rev.* 392 (1990). Professor Wasserman's criticism is the same move that act-utilitarians frequently make against rule-utilitarians to show that rule collapses into act, when Act-utilitarians say that individual violations of a rule do not amount to much loss of utility if they are not "publicized." Professor Luban says now that role morality and common morality cannot be balanced in a straightforward manner. Instead, the policy concerns of role should be recognized as deontological duties, the strength of which can still be determined by the Fourfold Root. They are not absolute duties, but they do occupy the default position morally; that is, usually one would do one's duty. This is a defeasible presumption that can be overridden by the requirements of common morality in exigent circumstances. (Policy can be understood as prima facie duties of the role agent, operating in a way similar to Ross' prima facie moral obligations.) Luban says this default position gives priority to the "social self," but it is difficult to understand how that is true except in the tautological sense that usually one would do one's duty. It seems to me that the moral role agent still has to jump out of the role into common morality to determine if duty is overridden in a particular situation by common morality, specifically by Professor Luban's "morality of acknowledgment" of people as people. Basically, Professor Luban has carved out an area in which we are free to do our role duties, but the area this is carved out from must be common morality. I hope this is not unfair, but I think Luban is still engaged in a straightforward balancing of role morality against common morality as before. He has just moved his thumb to the other side of the scale. In any event, his mid-course correction would not change my criticism of the standard conception of role morality because the primary criticism of it is that we have to jump out of our roles to discover what true morality is. Luban still has us doing that, even if it is less frequently. For an argument that "public" morality, as opposed to "private" morality, is necessarily more consequentialist, see Nagel, "Ruthlessness in Public Life" in *Public and Private Morality* (S. Hampshire ed. 1978) 75, reprinted in J. Callahan ed., *Ethical Issues in Professional Life* (Oxford: Oxford University Press 1988), 76.

14. By condemning Speer as an architect I do not mean that he failed in ways that might be called artistic, although it is true that he did. (The relationship between artistic failure of this sort and the failure I describe is surely a very complex one.) This is not what I mean by his failure to be a good architect, for there are many good architects who fail in artistic ways. For further discussion, see *infra* n. 43.

15. "Self-Deception," *supra* n. 3.

16. Speer says that he denied "my own past, my upper-middle-class origins, and my previous environment" when he joined the Nazi party. Speer, 20.

17. The expression is Eugene Davidson's, from Speer, Introduction, p. xviii.

18. Hauerwas and Burrell notice this as well. "Self-Deception," 92.

19. "This love for vast proportions was not only tied up with the totalitarian cast of Hitler's regime. Such tendencies, and the urge to demonstrate one's strength on all occasions, are characteristic of quickly acquired wealth. . . . Hitler's demand for huge dimensions, however, involved more than he was willing to admit to the workers. He wanted the biggest of everything to glorify his works and magnify his pride. These monuments were an assertion of his claim to world dominion long before he dared to voice any such intention even to his closest associates." Speer, 69.

20. Speer, 138.

21. Speer, 79.

22. Speer, 184.

23. Speer, 184.

24. Speer, 359, quoting Hitler.

25. Speer, 33. "The departure from reality, which was visibly spreading like a contagion, was no peculiarity of the National Socialist regime. But in normal circumstances people who turn their backs on reality are soon set straight by the mockery and criticism of those around them, which makes

them aware they have lost credibility. In the Third Reich there were no such correctives, especially for those who belonged to the upper stratum. On the contrary, every self-deception was multiplied as in a hall of distorting mirrors, becoming a repeatedly confirmed picture of a fantastical dream world which no longer bore any relationship to the grim outside world. In those mirrors, I could see nothing but my own face reproduced many times over. No external factors disturbed the uniformity of hundreds of unchanging faces, all mine." Speer, 291. Here Speer is telling us quite directly that rebellious ethics' concern with people reflecting upon themselves would not have worked for him.

26. David Kolb, *Postmodern Sophistications: Philosophy, Architecture and Tradition* (Chicago: University of Chicago Press, 1990), 2.

27. Speer, 19.

28. Speer, 32.

29. Speer, 523.

30. Speer, 523.

31. Speer, 159.

32. Speer, 291.

33. Speer, 375.

34. Eugene Davidson in Speer, Introduction, p. xviii.

35. Speer, 63.

36. Eugene Davidson in Speer, Introduction, p. xviii. Understanding this as a story of hubris ties Speer more closely to Marlowe's Faust. See Christopher Marlowe, *The Tragical History of the Life and Death of Doctor Faustus*. Rollo May describes Marlowe's Faust's hubris as "the refusal to accept the human role." Rollo May, *The Cry for Myth* (New York: Norton & Co., 1991) 231.

37. Would my argument be different if Speer's architectural work for Hitler had been better? What if we imagine a Speer whose work is recognized within the lasting community of architecture as beautiful? What if, despite Speer's corrupted motivations for his work, he accomplished the beautiful as an expression of the practical and the spiritual, as I have called it in the text? Speer could be a "successful" architect by the standards of the craft and yet be thoroughly despicable in the reasons he holds for his work as an architect.

But architecture not only teaches us what the beautiful in architecture is, it also teaches what it means to be a good architect, for it teaches that these are not the same. Being a good architect includes consideration of the motivation for your work. You can accomplish the beautiful in architecture by drawing upon the spiritual, but if your motivation is not toward the spiritual, your work is not your own. We may admire your work, but we do so because it expresses that which you are not.

As with Ananias and Sapphira's gifts to the early church (Acts 4:32–5:11), the good architecture of one not motivated rightly is a lie to God that takes the architect's own life and works from him. Notice that in the biblical story Ananias and Sapphira wanted to enjoy the position Barnabas had obtained by being a person for whom giving to the church was a way of life. They wanted the position he enjoyed, but were not willing to live by his example to obtain it. Their lives then lacked the integrity that would make them their own—an integrity we can understand only within the community of the early church. Our imaginary Speer, the one who does beautiful work, could not be a good architect because his life too would lack an integrity, one within the community of architecture.

Therefore, the standard in determining the good architect cannot be one of pure aesthetics—even if a pure aesthetic is possible, which I doubt that it is. This is easier to see for architecture than it is for other arts because no evaluation of architecture or the good architect can be separated from its social context.

38. "When I analyzed the complex of motives which so surprisingly led me back to this intimate circle, I realized that the desire to retain the position of power I had achieved was unquestionably a major factor. Even though I was only shining in the reflected light of Hitler's power—and I don't think I ever deceived myself on that score—I still found it worth striving for. I wanted, as part of his following, to gather some of his popularity, his glory, his greatness, around myself. Up to 1942, I still felt that my vocation as an architect allowed me a measure of pride that was independent of Hitler. But since then I had been bribed and intoxicated by the desire to wield pure power, to assign people to this and that, to say the final word on important questions, to deal with expenditures in the billions." Speer, 342.

One way of understanding my description of Speer as a Failed Architect is by comparing him with other architects. Can we imagine a Frank Lloyd Wright or even an I. M. Pei seeing architecture through the eyes of the leader of his government? Can we imagine a good architect defining success as an architect as Speer came to do so? Can we imagine Wright being an architect only because it could provide him with pride and position? I hope not and, if not, this is why Speer was a Failed Architect.

39. Here is Speer's description of Tessenow:

> Since my talent for drawing was inadequate, I was not accepted [into the advanced program.] In any case, I was beginning to doubt that I would ever make a good architect and took this verdict without surprise. Next semester Professor Heinrich Tessenow was appointed to the institute. . . .
>
> I promptly wrote to my fiancee: My new professor is the most remarkable, most clear-headed man I have ever met. I am wild about him and am working with great eagerness. He is not modern, but in a certain sense more modern than all the others. Outwardly he seems unimaginative and sober, just like me, but his buildings have something about them that expresses a profound experience. His intelligence is frighteningly acute. I mean to try hard to be admitted to his "master school" in a year, and after another year will try to become his assistant. Of course all this is wildly optimistic and is merely meant to trace what I'd like to do in the best of cases.
>
> Only half a year after completing my examination I became his assistant. In Professor Tessenow I had found my first catalyst—and he remained that for me until seven years later when he was replaced by a more powerful one. Speer, 11.

40. Speer, 11.

41. Speer, 27.

42. Speer's architectural staff could see Hitler quite differently, but he could not. Speer described one meeting of his architects with Hitler: "Neither the environment, with its innumerable generals, adjuncts, guard areas, barriers and passes, nor the aureole that this whole apparatus conferred upon Hitler, could intimidate these specialists. Their many years of successful practice of their professions gave them a clear sense of their rank and their responsibility. Sometimes the conversation developed into a heated discussion for they quite often forgot whom they were addressing" Speer, 232. Speer could not develop a sense of his rank and responsibility other than by never forgetting who Hitler was, for his rank and his responsibility did not grow out of architecture, but out of his being Hitler's architect. During conferences such as the one just described, Speer kept himself "in the background as far as possible" Speer, 232.

43. Speer, 49.

44. Speer, 79–80. For an excellent discussion of the metaphor of the hired gun in legal ethics, see Joseph Allegretti, "Have Briefcase Will Travel: An Essay on the Lawyer as Hired Gun," 24 *Creighton L. Rev.* 747 (1991).

45. *Id.* Several readers have commented that this delusion is typical of people in situations like that of Albert Speer. Such people believe they are having their say, but it is within such a limited area that having their say is of no real consequence. This is part of the way in which they feel used when they come to see their situation more truthfully.

46. Speer, 112.

47. This returns us to MacIntyre's point about the fact/value distinction serving the Manager's claims about the moral neutrality of expertise. *Supra,* n. 4. For more on the problems created by the fact/value distinction, see Stuart Hampshire, "Fallacies in Moral Philosophy," in Stanley Hauerwas and Alasdair MacIntyre, eds. *Revisions: Changing Perspectives in Moral Philosophy,* (Notre Dame: University of Notre Dame Press, 1983).

48. Speer, 120. Hitler understood the connection very well indeed. This is part of what made him so genuinely evil.

49. Interestingly, the first word Speer uses to describe Hitler in his chapter on him in the autobiography is "amateurishness." He says this was Hitler's dominant trait. "He never learned a profession and basically had always remained an outsider to all fields of endeavor." Speer, 230.

50. Speer, 198.

51. For rebellious ethics, what was a criticism of methodological reasoning and the bureaucracy it spawned became a criticism of all roles, including those defined by traditions of craftsmanship, such as architecture, as distortions of a true self. Rebellious ethics combined this concept of distortion with an assumption that it is the nature of all roles to undervalue the person *qua* person in moral decision-making. But, ironically, I believe it is this way of thinking about our roles that produces the bureaucratization of them. We should not apply a criticism originally directed at bureaucrats to crafts.

52. Speer, 173.

53. This morality served Speer well during the Nuremburg trials when he insisted that Hitler not be "whitewashed" or that the trials be used, as Goering wanted to use them, to promote a positive legend. Speer said: "I felt it was unethical to deceive the German people in this way; I also thought it dangerous because it would make the transition to the future more difficult

for the whole nation. Only the truth could accelerate the process of cutting free from the past" Speer, 511.

54. Speer, 60.

55. "The specifically modern self. . . finds no limits set to that on which it may pass judgment. . . . Everything may be criticized from whatever standpoint the self has adopted, including the self's choice of standpoint to adopt. It is in this capacity of the self to evade any necessary identification with any particular contingent state of affairs that some modern philosophers, both analytical and existentialist, have seen the essence of moral agency. To be a moral agent is, on this view, precisely to be able to stand back from any and every situation in which one is involved, from any and every characteristic that one may possess, and to pass judgment on it from a purely universal and abstract point of view that is totally detached from all social particularity. Anyone and everyone can thus be a moral agent, since it is in the self and not in social roles or practices that moral agency has to be located . . . " *After Virtue,* 31–32.

56. The shift to the roleless person hides the teleology while the role does not— the role's "why" is always a why about the ends of it. The "why" is about a teleology that is constantly being formed in a dialectic within the practice. The good X (architect, lawyer, doctor, etc.) requires constant creation of the role of X and, therefore, constant self-questioning. There is no good role which does not depend upon such an ongoing reflection upon itself and no good role whose teleology is not shaped by it. The settled teleology of the moment—that is, the way in which we now describe the role—is the one that has best resolved the constant dialectical arguments until the next opening in it appears. We understand the next change in the teleology historically and, therefore, there is a sense of direction to this teleology, one that we will continue to argue over. But in our talk of role moralities we often freeze the role, and thereby corrupt it, to one changeless teleology. See Richard Wasserstrom, "Lawyers as Professionals: Some Moral Issues," 5 *Human Rights J.* 76 (1975). It is only from this frozen perspective that conversation about role versus personal make any sense at all. It is a matter of convention for argument's sake and it is destroying a truthful understanding of the morality of roles.

57. There is a second, and closely related, way for rebellious ethics to answer this question about the self we are to take more seriously. If we are not to be self-deceived by our reflections, and if our lives are not to lose

coherence, we must try to make real this moral rebel—this "person who reflects." We must put flesh on the bare bones offered by rebellious ethics so that our faith is not in reflection alone but in a clearer image of who we are to become in our reflections. Those who practice professional ethics within the paradigm of rebellious ethics, however, seldom do this, and, I believe, for good reason. The self who lives rolelessly and, therefore, authentically—the self most compatible with a rebellion against role and a search for the broadest perspective possible—is a shallow romantic vision and the "move of a minor craftsman." As David Luban describes it:

> [A]lthough it may be "bad faith" to identify too closely with an occupational role, it is not less a distinct social role that withholds its commitment to a calling. Characteristically, that role is that of the adolescent, standing at life's crossroads with ideals too high for the compromises of professional roles—as well as a belief that his own "authenticity" is not to be sullied by the light of the public that darkens everything. David Luban, *Lawyers and Justice, An Ethical Study,* (Princeton: Princeton University Press 1988).

Thus, the "free and self aware individual" that Speer said would be our "counterpose to technology" becomes something like the James Dean of *Rebel Without a Cause.* As you can tell from the quotation, David Luban describes this as the Bohemian view held by those who live in the warehouse district and dress alike. But I do not think we can dismiss this romanticism so quickly, because much of the emotional appeal of rebellious ethics is charged by a James Dean version of Bohemia. James Dean does not live in the warehouse district. He is not countercultural; he is a rebel without a cause. Dean's morality is the morality of the loner and it has immense appeal in our culture.

Is this Romantic Rebel to be our counterbalance to the haunting moral failure of Speer the Pure Technician hovering above us as we go about our work as professionals?

Romanticism provides an acceptable personification for the self we must take more seriously, and a way of giving coherence to our lives as moral rebels, *because the Romantic Rebel has nothing to say.* The Romantic Rebel must be free of his past because in it are commitments that would deny to him the breadth of reflection and the rebellion by which he defines himself; he must be free of the future as well because to identify himself with a future is to accept yet another limiting commitment. But by freeing himself from the past and the future, the Romantic Rebel loses his ability to make himself intelligible to others or, for that matter, to himself. He becomes, like the Roleless Person, rebellious reflection without direction. He thinks that knowing the situation is all he needs to change it. In this Romantic Rebel we can see more clearly that reflection alone is surely not enough. Being able to reflect upon our professional roles as romantic rebels does not mean we will be able to criticize and to change.

And the Romantic Rebel, as Luban tells us, is just another perspective. He is just another preference of one way of life over others. Rebellious ethics, when it denies that this is so by holding on to this romantic embodiment of the Roleless Person, deceives us and leads us to a form of self-deception that is all its own. Most important, the price we pay for this romantic stance outside the system is, as it was for James Dean, a loss of what we would want to say to it.

For those of us concerned with Speer, Dean has nothing to say to the state—the defining body in which we find our roles embedded. James Dean is an attempt to give Aristotelian content to freedom and autonomy as moral ideals. He is a way to personify liberalism *and* to give content to the *authentic self* of some liberal and antiliberal thought. The problem with James Dean, however, is that, as Bob Dylan reminds us, "you've got to serve somebody." James Dean, the moral loner, does not live freely and, therefore, does not live more authentically, but lives instead in faithful service to freedom and autonomy. From Stanley Hauerwas and others we have learned that service to freedom and autonomy as moral ideals is, as a foundational matter, service to state. It seeks its moral resources there. In Dean's attempt to be free, he returns us by a circuitous route to a morality based upon and indistinguishable from the law and, therefore, Dean has nothing to say to the state for its laws speak for him as they did for Speer.

58. "Self-Deception," *supra,* n. 3.

59. "Self-Deception," 91–93.

60. Teachers of professional ethics constantly encounter one aspect of the problem of the moral rebel—the one Hauerwas and Burrell describe—although we seldom recognize it as such. It is there in the rapidly shifting postures of our students and ourselves as we respond to the varied problems of professional life from a variety of perspectives with expressions of little more than our own prejudices. As we respond, we often do so from perspectives and with prejudices that are profoundly at odds with one another. My students sometimes answer, as I do, as Southerners; sometimes as Georgians

or South Georgians; sometimes as Christians or Jews; sometimes as family; sometimes as lawyers; sometimes as gentlemen; sometimes as liberals; sometimes as students; and so on. This is what becomes of the moral rebel on whom our ethical rebellion depends because postmodern philosophy is correct and our deepest intuitions turn out not to be universal at all, but cultural and role-bound. Rather than finding one roleless moral rebel, we find, as our students do, that we are many people and that we occupy many roles. Who we are and which role we occupy as we address the problems of professional life is determined more as a reaction to the ways in which the various requirements of role are described and presented to us for moral consideration than as a reflection of any integrity in our own lives. Rebellious ethics' faith in reflection alone, then, is surely a bad faith because without a unifying understanding of the perspective from which we reflect and the teleology with which we reflect, and without some way of ordering our roles, it is very hard to understand how the product of our rebellious reflections could be anything other than the shifting prejudices of various points of view, or how these shifting prejudices could offer protection against self-deception.

61. This use of the term "master story" is from Michael Goldberg, *Jews and Christians, Getting Our Stories Straight: The Exodus and the Passion-Resurrection* (Philadelphia: Trinity Press International, 1991) pp. 13–15. By "master story" he meant "the kind of core foundational narrative that, in providing a community with its paradigmatic 'model of understanding the world. . . and guide for acting in it' (13), simultaneously gives rise to that community's most elementary, and often most distinctive, convictions about reality." See also Michael Goldberg, "God, Action, and Narrative: Which Narrative? Which Action? Which God?" *Journal of Religion*, 68, 1 (January 1988) 39–56, reprinted in Stanley Hauerwas and L. Gregory Jones, eds. *Why Narrative? Readings in Narrative Theology* (Grand Rapids: Eerdmans 1989) 348–365. The master story Hauerwas and Burrell have in mind is the Christian one. I do not, however, mean to limit my criticism of his use of master stories to religious ones although I am certainly open to the argument that only religious stories properly qualify under Goldberg's definition of the term. I wish, instead, to criticize the method by which Hauerwas and Burrell resort to master stories to provide a perspective for moral reflection outside the professional role, and I believe this particular criticism applies more broadly and includes secular ideologies such as Marxism that perhaps would not qualify definitionally as master stories.

62. "As one architectural assignment followed another, Speer had less and less reason to spell out the engagement he had begun. He knew what he was doing; he was an architect. No more was needed." And: "So Speer's new position [as Minister of Armaments] did not require him to rethink the master image of his life: he continued to be above all an architect." "Self-Deception," 92.

63. "Self-Deception," 93.

64. "Self-Deception," 94.

65. Speer falsely made himself the center of existence, as did Hitler. By doing so, he never became a true apprentice to the craft of architecture because architecture requires that the apprentice initially submit to the authority of the craft in order to become the type of person excellence in the craft requires one to be. See, Alasdair MacIntyre, *Three Rival Versions of Moral Enquiry* (Notre Dame: Univ. of Notre Dame Press, 1990) 51–81, for a description of this understanding of craft as Thomist and as emerging from the *Gorgias* and the *Republic.*

66. In MacIntyre's terms, we need to understand the potential moral reformation of Speer as something that could only arise within a dialectical test of competing traditions. Speer would have to become involved in a conversation in which the incoherencies of his self as Hitler's architect are revealed by their contrast with another tradition. This contrast could have afforded him the kind of self-knowledge essential to any determination of how his life is to be more adequately explained and accounted for. According to MacIntyre, there is no way to be engaged with a tradition other than on terms "framed with one eye to the specific character and history of that tradition on the one hand and the specific character and history of the particular individual. . . on the other." My claim in the text is that the specific character and history of Speer tells us that he could only be so engaged by such a conversation with the tradition of architecture. Alasdair MacIntyre, *Whose Justice? Which Rationality?,* 398.

67. In correspondence, Michael Goldberg has objected to my criticism that telling Speer the Christian story would have been pointless as being too concerned with efficacy. Taking a story to heart, he says, must be a matter of grace. We tell our stories to others, especially master stories, not because they work, but because they are true. Accordingly, the appropriate response to my criticism is: "So what?" And I agree. My point, however, is that Hauerwas and Burrell need to talk about Speer and not drift

to an abstraction for him in their resort to a master story. Speer was raised a Christian and, I suppose, there was some reason to believe that he would take this master story to be true. But thinking about it in this way ignores what Speer had done to himself. I think we must recognize that the only hope of Speer's moral salvation was in the last remains of God's beauty in his life—what he thought of as the spiritual in architecture. If grace is to come to Speer my guess is that it is to come this way; it is his way into the story. It is like the old joke about the woman stranded on the roof of her house in a flood refusing her rescuers three times because "God will save her." When she finally drowns and ask God why he let her do so, he says: "But I tried three times!" So, my response to Michael Goldberg must be that I, too, think it is in God's hands and a matter of grace. I just see his hands in a different place here. Obviously, the problem for me is to hold on to the God of Abraham in trying to see him at work in this way.

68. Speer, 339.

69. Speer, 344–45.

70. "Self-Deception," 86. Let me provide one simple example. I am a law professor, a lawyer, and a little league coach. If a friend needs to counsel me for my lawyering on the point that it is not whether you win or lose but how you play the game, they can do this best for me by reminding me that I am a little league coach. By making that connection for me, my friend would help me spell out my own self-deceptions because little league coaching within a community of good baseball people has given me some of the skill I need to see beyond the apparent seriousness of the moment.

71. Hauerwas and Burrell know that corrupt societies thrive on the virtues of the professions (as the Nazis, for example, thrived on the virtues of doctors) and they fear this. This is, however, also true of the church, in which their overarching narrative is kept alive if we look at the church with the same sociological eyes that we use to look at the professions. The virtues of architecture are not going to work if, working means stopping Hitler. All this means, however, is that architecture will not work in the way that Hitler has defined working.

72. The truth that Hauerwas speaks to medicine, for example, is the truth of medicine seen with his theological eyes. See Stanley Hauerwas, *Naming the Silences: God, Medicine, and the Problem of Suffering* (Grand Rapids: Eerdmans, 1990).

73. See Stanley Hauerwas, *Against the Nation: War and Survival In A Liberal Society* (San Francisco: Harper & Row, 1985).

74. These are, of course, the half-baked theological thoughts of an amateur theologian and you have been very kind to consider them.

75. I want to be as clear as I can that I have no quarrel with Hauerwas and Burrell's claims about Christianity as an example of a master story. I am a Christian, but I did not know what it meant to be one until I read Stanley Hauerwas. I just do not think that Hauerwas' claims about master stories have to conflict with our lives as professionals in the way he expresses it in the article I have relied upon here. Perhaps the real quarrel is whether or not professional roles can lead one to adequate stories. I believe they can; in fact, they may be the best way toward adequate stories we have left. In C.S. Lewis' terms, good architecture really is good on the road to Jerusalem. (My thanks to Tom Shaffer for this last point.)

Clergy Ethics:
Getting Our Story Straight

William H. Willimon

No ethic is worthy that does not require potentially the suffering of those we love. Nothing cuts against liberal ethical sentimentality more than this. We wish that there were some means of holding convictions without requiring the suffering of friends and families. We try to make "love" an individual emotion that does not ask someone else to suffer because of our love. . . . Pastors sometimes complain that it is unfair of the church to expect their children and spouses to make sacrifices because of the pastor's vocation. Of course, some of the sacrifices may be trivial and demeaning, arising from misunderstandings about ministry rather than from the nature of ministry. But the church should not be surprised that faithfulness to the gospel entails sacrifice. . . . Luther once commented that idolatry involves a question of what you would sacrifice your children for. The church has no quarrel with the sacrifice of children—except when such sacrifice is made to a false god. Our God is real, and makes real demands upon us. . . . God is about serious business. Any ethic worth having involves the tragic.[1]

This statement, from Stanley Hauerwas' and my book, *Resident Aliens*, caused a rumble among many clergy. Most mainline Protestant clergy, my brothers and sisters in ministry, desparately hope that there is some way to serve Jesus without hurting anybody. This has produced little more than the ethics of nice. Nice is what one must be when one hopes to be only a manager rather than a minister. If we won't allow Jesus to help us create a new world, then all we can do is manage the old one. Unfortunately for this brand of clergy ethics, the God who meets us in Jesus is about more serious business than being nice.

Pastors as Persons?

If any profession ought to know how to be ethical, it is the ordained ministry. Ministry and morality ought to be synonymous. Yet recent developments have rendered clergy ethics problematical. The thesis of this essay is that pastors have lost a sense of what they ought to do because we have forgotten who we are.[2]

Clergy are a peculiar species of the wider genus called Christian. Clergy have significance, not as some upper crust of Christian set over the lowly laity, not because they tend to be nicer than the average non-ordained Christian. Clergy are instrumental to what needs to happen in the church. Clergy cannot be regarded as "professionals" in the way the world speaks of doctors and lawyers. Clergy have no secret, marketable knowledge that is unavailable to everyone else in the church. They have few esoteric skills. This does not mean that clergy are powerless. Clergy are indeed powerful people who are ordained, under orders, to bear the faith of the church before the church, to preach the word, to administer the sacraments, to edify the congregation through preaching, teaching, and pastoral care. Clergy are interesting only as a function of what God intends to do in the church. Therefore, clergy ethics arise from the peculiar nature of clergy.[3] Clergy ethics have few epistemological allies in the world of ethics, are illuminated by few observations which are relevant to generic "professional ethics." Being a pastor is an ethical challenge because one has been called to be a *pastor*.

I therefore disagree with many contemporary critics of Christian ministry who assume that present-day pastors suffer from some sort of personal problem—they are too overworked, or have too little self-esteem, or lack sufficient self-assertion. While much of that may be true of contemporary clergy, none gets to the heart of how frightening it is to be a pastor empowered in service to Jesus Christ and his church.

In his popular book on caring for clergy who care, *The Pastor As Person,* Gary Harbaugh says that "most difficulties pastors face in the parish arise when the pastor forgets that he or she is a person."[4] Contrary to Harbaugh, I believe the ethical troubles occur when pastors forget that they are pastors.

Many contemporary commentators on Christian ministry, like Harbaugh, tell clergy that only by being "in touch" with the common humanity which they share with their parishioners—their femaleness, maleness, empathy, need for love, or whatever personal attribute is considered worthy by the commentator—can pastors be up to the demands of ministry. Some of the worst damage that pastors do to their parishioners, they say, is done in the name of theology, or tradition, or church discipline. As a pastor said to me recently, "Theology is fine, but for most of the problems people bring to me, I just have to do what I think is right. That's what people want from me, compassion and care." Or, as Harbaugh claims, a pastor ought never forget that he or she is a person.

This attitude is a strange view of a "person." Where is this "person" who can somehow be detached from commitments, society, history, economics? A pastor is a person who has had hands laid upon his or her head, made public promises before God and the church, willingly yoked his or her life to the demands of the gospel and the people the gospel gathers.

Pastors are not called to care, but to care "in Jesus' name." How can this marvelously caring and empathetic pastor, who has subordinated church tradition, theology, and ordination to the needs of his or her own personality, be sure that his or her care is not another means of self-deception (what we once called *sin*)?

On the Dangers of Being a Caring Pastor

A pastor's glowing account of his own struggle to be caring and compassionate with a parishioner illustrates the problem.[5] Mr. Lord, Pastor of Rush Creek Christian Church, Arlington, Texas, describes

his dilemma as a problem of pastoral care. I see his narrative as one of
moral confusion.

Do I Have To Forgive?

I was asked by Betty Jane Spencer, "Preacher, do I have to forgive a man
who murdered my four sons?"

A few years earlier, a group of young men had gotten high on drugs and
broken into her Indiana farmhouse and committed mass murder. Betty
Jane's sons were killed. She was shot and left for dead. Since beginning his
prison sentence, one of the convicted criminals wrote to tell her he had
"found Christ" and asked for her forgiveness.

When she said "Preacher," I knew she wanted more than my opinion.
She wanted a statement that represented the Christian tradition. "Am I obligated as a Christian to forgive in this situation? Just what does the church
mean by 'forgiveness'? He did not say 'I'm sorry' . . . just 'Forgive me,'"
she continued. "What am I to do?"

I told her to give me six months and I would try to give her an answer.
During that time I sought out victims of violent crimes, and those whose
loved ones have been shattered by crimes. I studied the Jewish tradition and
looked at what the church has said.

The victims who talked with me were very disturbed by the issue of
forgiveness. They were constantly being told they must forgive, but most
could not. . . .

Victims' resistance to forgiveness seems to focus on two elements: forgiveness as forgetting and forgiveness as excuse. . . . Victims of violence
are deeply concerned that their loved one not be forgotten.

Forgiving may also imply excusing. . . . Does finding Christ excuse
what was done? . . . Leaders of the prison ministry say that man should
be released so he can witness for Christ. Betty Jane wonders why he can't
witness for Christ in prison.

What can we learn from the Judeo-Christian tradition about forgiveness
which does not imply forgetting or excusing? On Yom Kippur, sins against
God are forgiven. But if you have sinned against your neighbor, you must
go to him or her and seek forgiveness. Not even God forgives what you
have done to another. . . .

I remembered the times I have proclaimed, "Your sins are forgiven." I
now imagine a battered wife thinking to herself, "Who gave you the right

to forgive the one who beats me?" I no longer say in a general or public way, "Your sins are forgiven."

. . . Victims ask us not to demand that they themselves pronounce absolution. Those of us who speak on behalf of the Christian community can speak of God's mercy to the truly repentant, but we have no right to insist that the victim establish a relationship with his or her victimizer to effect a reconciliation. Even without some reconciliation with the perpetrator, most victims can gradually "let go" of their hate, anger, rage or despair. Their negative energy becomes channeled into constructive activity such as working for victim causes or supporting other victims.

Betty Jane Spencer is open to a future without her sons. She is a prominent national leader in the victim rights movement, currently the Florida state director of Mothers Against Drunk Driving. But she is not open to a future with those who killed her children. She had no relationship with them before the murders and she desires none now. She hopes they create for themselves a positive future, but one that does not include her.

Betty Jane is quite ready to affirm that God is merciful and is hopeful that the murderers of her sons will find a genuine relationship with God. But don't ask her to be responsible for their salvation. Don't ask her to go to them and judge their hearts. Let a representative of the church assume that burden.

When I saw Betty Jane six months later, I told her No.

Lord presents himself as a pastor who, confronted by a specific, suffering parishioner, empathetically struggled with her situation in a caring, compassionate way.[6] Some pastors, when asked by this woman, "Do I have to forgive?" might have quoted scripture to her, not because Jesus was an "expert," but because Jesus is the one who brought Pastor Lord and Betty Jane Spencer together in the first place. Jesus certainly had much to say on the subject of forgiveness, much of which was very straightforward and specific: "And forgive us our debts, as we have also forgiven our debtors" (Mt. 6:12).

Lord was too deeply concerned for this woman to quote any Jesus to her. So he went rummaging in the "Judeo-Christian tradition"[7] for answers and, after six months, found the answer that she really need not try to forgive the young killer who asked her forgiveness. That was not her vocation as a Christian, nor was it Pastor Lord's "right" to urge her to do so.

Considering how hot a topic forgiveness has been throughout the history of the church, it is interesting that Lord found little help from scripture, the church fathers, or his own denomination. Now that he has helped himself to a deeper understanding of the matter, he even finds that he can no longer speak of blanket forgiveness in his liturgical leadership of his congregation.

I suppose that Betty Jane Spencer should be grateful that her pastor is such a caring person. Other pastors might have quoted scripture to her, demanded that she not receive the Eucharist until she had made peace with this estranged brother (Mt. 5:21–26), publicly asked the church to pray for her to help her make this very tough move in her life, encouraged her to meet with them for the next couple of months to pray about the matter, or some other uncaring, traditional action.

Clergy and Rebellious Ethics

In his decision to be empathetic, to eschew tradition, scripture, and the resources of the church, Pastor Lord represents what Jack L. Sammons, Jr. has in the previous chapter called "rebellious ethics." Like the story that has been constructed about Albert Speer, we pastors have devised a narrative that "we must stand apart from our professional roles in personal moral judgment of them." The worst moral danger, according to the paradigm of rebellious ethics, is for lawyers or pastors to be "captured by their professional roles." The goal of this ethic is to have no ethic imposed upon us by our role, to be the sort of pastor who can be a pastor without taking him or herself too seriously or, as Gary Harbaugh put it, who can be more a person than a pastor.

The more we summon up the psychological courage to rebel against our socially-imposed roles, the more ethical we will be, says rebellious ethics. The cynicism within the conversation of the Ministers' Monday Morning Coffee Hour, in which clergy sit around making cutting comments about their flocks or regale one another with sacrilegious jokes, represents a rather harmless attempt at ersatz rebellion from the clerical roles they find so confining, an attempt to deny clerical power by making fun of being a cleric. Pastor Lord's attempt to rebel against his ecclesially-sanctioned role is more heroic, and therefore more dangerous. We clergy know enough about our roles to know that they put us in risky positions where power is being used and therefore potentially abused, but we know not enough how to change our professional practices to improve our profession.

Rather than engage in deep reflection on the subtleties of the exercise of power in our roles, we adopt the stance of the romantic rebel, the fiction of the roleless person. Rebellious ethics assumes that it is the nature of all roles to undervalue the person as a *person* engaged in moral decision-making. However, in deciding to fall back on his own resources, to rebel against traditional expectations for pastors, I believe that Pastor Lord may have offered Betty Jane Spencer less rather than more. Now recast by her pastor into the role of the romantic moral loner, Betty Jane Spencer becomes an example of Richard Rorty's Kantian divinized self.[8] Ironically, this pastor has not rebelled against his socially-assigned role; rather, he has fallen backward into the clutches of the dominate cultural function of clergy in our day—the care, encouragement, and detachment of the individual psyche from any commitment other than dedication to the self.[9]

As Martin Marty notes, American clergy function within a national polity in which the Constitution decreed early on in our national life that "religion had to be put in a legally subordinate situation in civil life, where so many ethical decisions are made."[10] Despite Marty's optimism that "to make religion legally subordinate does not mean that the state can render the clergy morally subservient," Pastor Lord's case suggests that it has. The state has made, through the Constitution, individuals of us all, telling us that we have thereby been given the maximum amount of freedom through detachment from family, tradition, community, or history. The genius of this liberal constitutional arrangement is that, while telling us we are free, the modern state has found how much easier detached individuals are to manage than people who have a home, or a tribe, or a neighborhood, or a past.

Marty is right in his answer to his question, "What does this have to do with clergy ethics? It means that ministers . . . have the most direct effect on private and personal life. They have a measure of unimpeded influence on those who choose to affiliate with the religious body they serve. They also find themselves 'boxed in,' segregated as it were, in the private sphere. 'Religion is a private affair' is an effective way of cutting off the influence of clergy ethics. . . . To introduce a religious back-drop or argument appears to be an intrusion into the civil fabric."[11] The pastor compensates for this lack of public significance by becoming the eager chaplain to the dominant ethic: you stay out of my life and I'll stay out of yours. The "genius" of the contemporary pastor is that he or she attempts to achieve public power by being nice—appearing to be caring, empathetic, and kind—while conveying this culture's official sanctioned ethic: there is no point to life other than that which you personally devise. You stay out of my life and I'll stay out of yours.

So in our willingness to keep things private and personal, detached from ecclesial demands, in exchange for our alleged religious freedom, clergy have not rebelled against cultural expectations. We have acquiesced into the most ethically debilitating of those expectations. It is not that we have been too good at being pastors and not good enough at being people; rather, we have not been good enough at being pastors. True morality—the ability to judge our own self-deception, the gift of seeing things in perspective—comes from practices outside those sanctioned by the system. It comes from being forced, Sunday after Sunday, to lead and to pray the Prayer of Confession followed by the Words of Absolution. It comes from being ordered, Sunday after Sunday, to "Do this in remembrance of me." Our extravagant claim is that through obedience to these practices, Jesus gives us the resources we need to be faithful disciples. And we will never know whether or not Jesus was speaking truthfully if our pastors refuse to hold us accountable to Jesus' demands. Our aim as pastors is to produce the sort of people whose lives will make Jesus appear either to be incredibly crazy ("Love your enemies, pray for those who persecute you"—Mt. 5:44) or amazingly able to produce the sort of people he demands ("To you has been given the Kingdom"—Mk. 4:11).

During a recent lunch the chair of our chemistry department noted that ministers could profit by the ethics of chemists. "The ethics of chemists?" I asked. "Sure. It is impossible to be a good chemist and a liar at the same time. The chemist's honesty about experimental results, openness with other chemists, commitment to standard methodology would enhance the practice of ministry." Which suggests that Jack Sammons is correct. We don't need to be better rebels from the virtues and practices of our craft; we need to be more deeply linked to them. As I think Pastor Lord demonstrates, the irony is that by acting independently, thinking for ourselves, standing on our own two feet, we have not rebelled against the system; we have capitulated into the worst aspects of it. I recall the United Methodist district superintendent who bragged that he thought it most important that a district superintendent "not take himself too seriously." Sammons' essay suggests that he should take himself, *as a district superintendent,* very seriously. Separated from the skills and commitments of our craft, we are left morally exposed, victims of conventional wisdom. For pastors—particularly pastors who are also district superintendents—the worst form of self-deception may be the deceptive idea that we are without power, just one of the boys, not taking ourselves too seriously, simply a person.

Consider the ethics of preaching. The disciplines required by the craft of sermon preparation—self-criticism, obedience to the text, confidence in the congregation, weekly hard work—are disciplines which are more moral than technical or personal. In fact, that may be a good test whether or not ordinands are morally ready to be entrusted with a congregation: Have they mastered the craft well enough to write fifty-two Sundays of sermons without lying too often?

The notion that we are most fully ourselves, most fully ethical when we have freed ourselves from the demands of scripture, tradition, and church merely demonstrates the power of the socially-sanctioned story that holds us captive. As George Lindbeck noted, we are all liberals.[12] That is, the individual is the basic unit of reality, the sole center of meaning. We are all children of modernity, that story which holds that each of us has a right, a duty, to be free of all stories save the ones we have individually chosen. This is Peter Berger's "heretical imperative,"[13] the modern conceit that we are free to determine our own destinies, that we have no fate other than the fate we choose. In earlier times, heresy was that way of thinking in which a person chose what to believe rather than believed what he or she had been told. Today, we are all fated to be heretics in that we all live under the modern presupposition that none of us should be held to commitments which we have not freely chosen. Our morality has thus made freedom of choice an absolute necessity. Freedom has become the fate of the individual. If I explain my actions on the basis of tradition, community standards, my parents' beliefs, scripture, I have obviously not thought things through (for six months, like Pastor Lord!), have not decided for myself, have not been true to myself, have not rebelled against the external imposition of a role, so I have not been moral.[14]

As Stanley Hauerwas has shown repeatedly, this mode of thinking is but another form of deception, enslavement to a story (the Enlightenment myth of the free individual) which tells us that it is possible to choose our own stories. We have merely exchanged narrative masters. Pastor Lord has jettisoned the older, traditional story that it is my duty as an ordained leader of the church to bear the church's tradition before my congregation for a more socially acceptable one: my duty is to my individual feelings and standards in order to free my parishioners to be dutiful to their individual feelings and standards. The modern world said, That's only a story. The postmodern world has realized, There's only story. So the question is not, Shall our lives be narratively constructed? but, Which narrative shall form our lives?[15]

Pastor Lord acts as if he is freeing himself and then his parishioner from an oppressive, naive, traditional story—that we Christians have a duty to forgive people who wrong us, even when they don't deserve it. In reality, the episode as narrated by Pastor Lord shows how difficult it is for modern liberal societies to acknowledge the subtle forms of coercion that hold them together because they derive their legitimation from the presumption that there is no moral authority more significant than the individual conscience. Believing this to be true, Pastor Lord is able to dismiss scripture, Jesus, church tradition, and the liturgy of the church in favor of the freedom to do what he thinks personally to be right.

He even dismisses the feelings of his parishioner. The possibility of forgiveness, which initially troubles her so deeply that she seeks out the counsel of her pastor, is explained away in a barrage of anxious pastoral reading and reflection. There is no exploration of the possibility that perhaps the woman's concern is a legitimate expression of her disciple-ship. How does the pastor know that she is incapable of the radical action which Jesus demands? Who told the pastor that he was responsible for protecting the woman from radical action like forgiving her enemies?

Why doesn't he at least ask her, "What does forgiveness mean to you?" Perhaps she has an inadequate notion of Christian forgiveness, thinking it to be a facile pat on the head or moral amnesia. Pastor Lord acts as if he has graciously sidestepped issues of power and authority, thrusting the is-sue back upon Betty Jane Spencer after reporting on his six months of re-search. Yet one is intrigued by the subtle but powerful ways he continues to define the situation for her. Power has been wrenched away from church tradition and scripture and reduced to an exchange between an individual pastor and his parishioner. Nothing is more insidiously power-ful than people who think they have no power.

In responding to a barrage of letters critical to this article, Lord said: "At times we do our theology standing on our biblical tradition, but at other times we do our theology standing beside those in pain. . . . We must also stand with those who are hurting and let their pain define what we shall do and who we shall be. We do not define them. They define us."[16] Aside from questions about a theology which lets "hurting" and "pain" define us and our sisters and brothers, one notes Pastor Lord's inability to see how Betty Jane Spencer's questions did not define him. He defined her.

What the pastor presents as a case of exemplary, empathetic pastoral care might be seen as an abdication of pastoral responsibility in favor of the exercise of purely personal power. Is protection and care of the woman his goal or is *self*-protection more important? Her question, "Preacher, do I have to forgive?" raises threatening questions. Was Jesus crazy? Are the words of Jesus relevant only for Jesus who forgave his enemies (Lk. 23:34), or perhaps a saint like Stephen who forgave his murderers (Acts 7:60), but not for his ordinary disciples? How does Pastor Lord know if his response arises out of his pastoral compassion or out of his participation in the modern control of people by managers who control people precisely by reassuring them that through manage-rial niceness they are being allowed to be individuals? By the end of the story, there is no one left in the story except Pastor Lord and Betty Jane Spencer. Mrs. Spencer, once a tragic victim of violence, continues as a victim, though now as a "national leader in the victim rights movement." She becomes a professional victim, a person defined solely by pain and hurt. This is precisely the end of the story Jesus sought to avoid with his instructions to mourners, the hungry, and the persecuted in his Sermon on the Mount. The ethic there is not to produce and perpetuate victims, but rather to urge the means of enabling victims to be victorious over their victimizers through forgiveness, blessing, and prayer.

What sort of church would be required to have a member seriously ask, "Preacher, do I have to forgive?" Pastor Lord implies that he and his church are now so sensitive to the plight of battered spouses and wronged women that he now no longer works for reconciliation and forgiveness, no longer dares to ask God for reconciliation in worship. What he may mean is that our church is already so lacking in sources of power outside our own psyches, our leaders so devoid of any moral authority beyond whether or not they are nice and we happen to like them, our worship so bereft of liturgical resources (like the Catholic Rite of Reconciliation), that we are now unable to make big, countercultural moves in our lives. We can no longer afford to have people running around loose asking, "Preacher, do I have to forgive?"[17]

One of the gifts of historical reflection, subservience to tradition, and participation in the liturgy is conversation with a *polis* outside ourselves. The tradition of the church has a way of raising the political, communal power question for the church. Rather than see Betty Jane's question as an opportunity for community soul-searching, the pastor quickly assures her this is a personal matter, nothing which might potentially involve the whole church, nothing which might require a reexamination of pastoral style and substance, but something just between the two of us. Nothing political.[18] In the end, Betty Jane is abandoned to her hate, her hurt. Perhaps even more tragic for the baptized, the church is also abandoned to be a conglomeration of isolated individuals who muddle through as best they individually can, with little responsibility to the Betty Jane Spencers of the world.

What sort of pastor would I have to be to answer this woman with "Yes, I really think Jesus means for you to be the sort of person who can forgive even an enemy so great as the man who killed your sons"? What set of ecclesial practices and internal disciplines would need to be developed? What sort of preacher would I need to be to craft sermons which would give this woman the courage to be as radical as Jesus seems to demand? Without consideration of these congregational disciplines and pastoral resources, the teachings of Jesus are unintelligible and we are all abandoned by the church and its clergy to "making up our own minds" on matters as serious as forgiveness, as if our minds were all that mattered.

A couple of years ago, reading through the work of John Wesley, founder of the Methodist movement in eighteenth-century England, I was impressed by how important for Wesley was that rather outrageous statement by Jesus at the end of his Sermon on the Mount (Mt. 5:48), in which Jesus tells his people to "Be perfect, therefore, as your heavenly Father in heaven is perfect."[19]

That was a central text for Wesley. Taking that text with utter seriousness, he asked not, Did Jesus really mean these words in this way? Or, Why would a nice person like Jesus say something impossible like that to earnest people like us? Rather, Wesley said, in effect, What sort of church and church leaders would be required to produce people who could be perfect as their Father in heaven is perfect? He knew that it would not be the established Church of England. It must be a church in which people knew the cost of discipleship and were encouraged to pay. It would be a church of much grace and forgiveness, for it would be a church with a huge amount of sin, given its desire to be perfect.

Wesley invented something new: small groups of persons bound together for prayer, singing, mutual correction, and forgiveness. He thus made ordinary eighteenth-century English people into saints on the basis of his insight that Christian morality is inherently communal, corporate. Not as individuals, but only as a group are people able to summon the courage, the honesty to forgive.

Lacking the kind of bold, risky, political, creativity of a John Wesley, all we can do is service the status quo, be chaplains to the present order, urge people to think deeply, feel sincerely, and make up their own minds. Clergy are thus fated to be nice. Nobody will get hurt doing that. Of course, nobody will get saved either. Nobody will get to be a saint.

Stanley Hauerwas called my attention to a book by Charles Taylor, *Sources of the Self: The Making of Modern Identity*. Taylor notes that most of the classical moralists—Aristotle, Plato, the Stoics—taught that the moral life was inherently hierarchical. Good morality required a class of elites who had the time and the ability to engage in the higher activities of contemplation and ethical discernment.[20] Modernity has leveled everything, believing that the good life is inherently available to everyone regardless of status, training, or ability. There were many reasons for this leveling: democracy, secularism, the rise of science. For our purposes, Taylor says that the Protestant Reformation is an important source of modern confusion about requirements for the moral life.

The Reformation rejected the notion of ecclesial mediation of divine grace, the historic Catholic presumption that some within the Body of Christ could be more dedicated to the faith and thus more capable of winning merit and salvation than others. Now everyone is a saint. Salvation is an exclusive, utterly unmerited gift of a gracious God. God is no more present through specially dedicated people than God is present through everyone. Thus the Reformation made its own distinctive contribution to the individualism of the modern world. Now that salvation was no longer mediated by the church, its clergy, or its saints, the personal commitment of the individual believer became the basic unit of the faith. Participation in the church's worship, the mediating power of the sacraments as means of grace, was jettisoned in favor of the disposition of the individual believer. Whereas Catholicism taught that "I am a passenger on the ecclesial ship on its journey to God. . . . Protestantism [implied] there can be no passengers. . . . There is no ship in the catholic sense, no common movement carrying humans to salvation. Each believer rows his or her own boat."[21]

After the Reformation, vocation, which had earlier usually meant a call to the priesthood or the monastic life, became any employment which claimed to be useful to the common good of humanity. Vocation became having a job. Revelation, for the Puritans, became a twofold matter of "rebelling against a traditional authority which was merely feeding on its own errors and as a returning to the neglected sources: the Scriptures on the one hand, experimental reality on the other. Both appealed to what they saw as living experience against dead received doctrines—the experience of personal conversion and commitment, and that of direct observation of nature's workings."[22]

The main arbiter in Pastor Lord's deliberations has now become experimental reality. Even the scriptures, which were important for the Puritans, have been jettisoned because they are judged by the only source of revelation now to be trusted: our personal experience of what seems right.

As Hauerwas notes, one of the extraordinary aspects of Taylor's analysis is the way in which he shows how the Reformation's effort to deny special mediation of God's grace through peculiar institutions or special people ultimately destroyed the church's christological center. Earlier, the church had to deal somehow with troublesome statements by Jesus such as forgiving one another seven times seven times (Mt. 18:21–22). By the time we arrive at Pastor Lord, Jesus himself has been rendered so ordinary that there is no need even to explain him away. Jesus is no more revelatory that Pastor Lord's personal experience. Everything is ordinary. Having disposed of the extraordinary possibility of miracle, creation, or divine intervention in history, there is now no longer the possibility of extraordinary moral demand because extraordinary moral demand exists only in an ecology of extraordinary possibility for change, conversion. Everything is flattened to "what seems right to me."

So the discussion between pastor and parishioner occurs in the abstract, as if there were no church. Nothing is asked of the church, as if Lord realized that everyone in the church would see this woman's dilemma as her personal problem. There is no reaching out to the church as the sort of people who might enable ordinary people to make extraordinary moves in their lives. Is there no one else in the congregation who has ever had an enemy? There is no mention that this woman is baptized, a person who is pledged to live under the sign of the cross; nor is there any mention that she lives among the baptized, people who are pledged to provide the support necessary, not for her to be happy, but to be faithful. Sentimentality is the best such ethics can deliver.

The Ordained as Those under Orders

It is not necessary for Pastor Lord self-righteously to tell Betty Jane Spencer that she ought to forgive her enemies. Rather, it is necessary for those who are ordained to witness to the faith of the church, to recall what it means to be Christian in life's circumstances, and to remind the church what it means to be God's answer to what ails the world. Of course, we pastors are smart enough to know that if we told someone like Betty Jane Spencer to take the teachings of Jesus seriously, she might turn and ask us when was the last time we took Jesus with such seriousness, and then where would we be?

Perhaps well on our way to a recovery of the disciplines of discipleship.

To be a Christian is to be someone who is baptized into those practices and virtues based upon the claim that in Jesus Christ God is busy saving the world, not on our terms, but on God's terms. Christians claim to have a truthful account of the way the world is put together.[23]

When we jettison our language,[24] our peculiar way of relating to the world by such odd practices as praying for and forgiving enemies, we testify to our adoption of a counter-account of the way the world is. For the world is quite right in judging the truth of our convictions on the basis of the lives we are able to produce.

The Right Story

Ian Bedlow, hero of Anne Tyler's novel, *Saint Maybe,* stumbles into the little storefront Church of the Second Chance. Ian is a college freshman. He had not intended to say anything during the service, but somehow during the prayer time he blurted out his dark secret before the little congregation and Reverend Emmett:

> In a voice not quite his own, Ian said, "I caused my brother to, um, kill himself."
>
> Reverend Emmett gazed at him thoughtfully.
>
> "I told him his wife was cheating on him," Ian said in a rush, "and now I'm not even sure she was. I mean I'm pretty sure she did in the past, I know

I wasn't totally wrong, but. . . . So he drove into a wall. And then his wife died of sleeping pills and I guess you could say I caused that too, more or less. . . ."

"So it looks as if my parents are going to have to raise the children," Ian said. Had he mentioned there were children? "Everything's been dumped on my mom and I don't think she's up to it—her or my dad, either one. I don't think they'll ever be the same, after this. And my sister's busy with her own kids and I'm away at college most of the time. . . ." "So anyhow," he said, "that's why I asked for that prayer. . . . don't you think I'm forgiven?"

"Goodness, no," Reverend Emmett said briskly.

Ian is shocked. "I thought God forgives everything." Reverend Emmett agrees but then adds, "You can't just say, 'I'm sorry God.' . . . You have to offer reparation—concrete, practical reparation. . . ."

Ian countered, "But what if there isn't any reparation? What if it's something nothing will fix?" Reverend Emmett responded that Jesus "helps us do what you can't undo. But only after you've tried to undo it." Reverend Emmett told Ian to "see to the children."

"Okay. But . . . see to them in what way, exactly?"

"Why, raise them, I suppose."

"Huh?" Ian said. "But I'm only a freshman!"

Reverend Emmett turned to face him, hugging the stack of hymnals against his concave shirt front.

"I'm away in Pennsylvania most of the time," Ian told him.

"Then maybe you should drop out."

"Drop out?"

"Right."

Ian stared at him.

"This is some kind of test, isn't it?" he said finally.

Reverend Emmett nodded, smiling. Ian sagged with relief.

"It's God's test," Reverend Emmett told him.

"So. . . ."

"God wants to know how far you'll go to undo the harm you've done."

"But He wouldn't really make me follow through with it," Ian said.

"How else would He know, then?"

"Wait," Ian said. "You're saying God would want me to give up my education. Change all my parents' plans for me and give up my education."

"Yes, if that's what's required," Reverend Emmett said.

"But that's crazy! I'd have to be crazy!"

"'Let us not love in word, neither in tongue,'" Reverend Emmett said, "'But in deed and in truth.' First John three, eighteen."

"I can't take on a bunch of kids! Who do you think I am? I'm nineteen years old!" Ian said. "What kind of a cockeyed religion is this?"

"It's the religion of atonement and complete forgiveness," Reverend Emmett said. "It's the religion of the Second Chance."

Then he set the hymnals on the counter and turned to offer Ian a beatific smile. Ian thought he had never seen anyone so absolutely at peace.[25]

Before the novel ends, Ian's act of atonement, following Reverend Emmett's call to "see to the children," leads to his reconciliation with God and with himself. Ian is changed through a little storefront church of loving misfits and a pastor who dared to preach the gospel. Maybe Ian even becomes a saint. Ian has wandered into a community where forgiveness is a central practice, whose church and pastor have adapted themselves to Jesus' demand to forgive rather than adapting the demand of Jesus to the social status quo. This is the story which must ignite the imaginations of pastors if we are to be better than we would have been if we had been left to our own devices. Alas, the narrative of rebellious ethics, exemplified in Pastor Lord's account of Betty Jane Spencer, has captured us.

Recently, a group of Christian and Jewish ethicists and theologians issued a formidable group of essays, *Clergy Ethics In A Changing Society*.[26] As a whole, the volume is a testimonial to the frequently heard charge that today's clergy have little idea of who they are and no clue about what they are supposed to be doing. Generally speaking, clergy ethics is described in these essays as a personality disorder among pastors, with little reference to church, scripture, or tradition. Exceptions are the essays by William May on "Images of the Minister" and Rebecca S. Chopp on "Liberating Ministry." Chopp's essay is interesting mainly because she is a liberation theologian and her essay therefore has a point of view and some unashamed commitments which give her interesting opinions about our allegedly "changing society." On the whole, though, this book typifies why clergy today are in trouble.

None of the essays in *Clergy Ethics* refers to the rites of ordination, a curious fact since, if one wants to know who clergy are and what they are supposed to be doing, one might consult those ecclesial statements made to and about clergy when the church ordained them. The lack of reference to rites of ordination is not so curious when one considers that most of the essays in *Clergy Ethics* envision pastors doing their work in much the same fashion as Pastor Lord. Martin Marty's title for his essay typifies the problem: "Ministers On Their Own."

Clergy ethics would do well to attend more closely to the story of Reverend Emmett than to that of Pastor Lord. For in that story of a wise and obedient pastor's courage to confront a young man's life, supported and enacted within an odd and faithful storefront church, we see ministry as it is meant to be narrated.[27] That story is the one elicited from the ordinal of the church. When someone is ordained as a leader of the church, hands are laid upon the person's head, a gesture of giving and receiving power and of vesting with the community's authority, which should be the basis of anything we say about clergy ethics. The significance of that gesture is made explicit in the prayer at the conclusion of the Methodist service of ordination:

> Gracious God,
> Give to these your servants the grace and power they need
> to serve you in this ministry,
> so that your people may be strengthened
> and your name glorified in all the world.
> Make them faithful pastors, patient teachers, and wise counselors.
> Enable them to serve without reproach,
> to proclaim the gospel of salvation,
> to administer the Sacraments of the new covenant,
> to order the life of the Church,
> and to offer with all your people
> spiritual sacrifices acceptable to you;
> through Jesus Christ our Lord,
> who lives and reigns with you,
> in the unity of the Holy Spirit,
> one God, now and for ever. Amen.[28]

NOTES

1. Stanley Hauerwas and William H. Willimon, *Resident Aliens: Life in the Christian Colony* (Nashville: Abingdon, 1989), 148–49.

2. See Stanley Hauerwas, "Clerical Character," 133–248, for a concise critique of ministerial "professionalism" from the standpoint of Hauerwas's ethics of character, in his *Christian Existence Today* (Durham, NC: Labyrinth Press, 1988). I hope that my treatment of clerical ethics is complementary to that of Hauerwas.

3. Jackson Carroll clarifies the peculiar nature of pastoral power, what Carroll calls "legitimate authority" in "Some Issues in Clergy Authority," *Review of Religious Research,* Vol. 23, No. 2, Dec. 1981, 99–208: "Authority of office reflects the religious group's concern to protect the sanctity of its tradition, preserving the charisma and, teaching of its founder(s) by institutionalizing them into an office. . . ."

    The *locus classicus* for beginning to consider the Christian ministry, at least from a mainline Protestant perspective, is H. Richard Niebuhr, *The Purpose of the Church and Its Ministry* (New York: Harper and Row, 1956).

4. Gary Harbaugh, *The Pastor as Person* (Minneapolis: Augsburg, 1984), 9. The Academy of Parish Clergy voted this book "the most useful book for pastors" in the year that it was published.

5. "Do I Have To Forgive?," *The Christian Century,* Oct. 9, 1991, 902–3.

6. Alasdair MacIntyre, in *After Virtue* (Notre Dame, IN: University of Notre Dame Press, 1981), demonstrated how the modern claim of expertise, combined with the illusion of value neutrality, led to professional ethics as we know it. He also showed the subtle manipulative qualities behind such detached, expert neutrality. See *After Virtue,* 72–74. See also Stanley M. Hauerwas and William H. Willimon, "Ministry As More Than A Helping Profession," *The Christian Century,* March 15, 1989, 282–84.

7. Long ago, Michael Goldberg convinced me that the phrase "Judeo-Christian" makes sense only as a liberal perversion of the testimony of both Jews and Christians. Pastor Lord's appeal to this allegedly common tradition demonstrates this. Yom Kippur is not a universal idea which makes sense for everybody. Rather, Yom Kippur is the name for a whole set of practices of a specific people, just as the Catholic Rite of Reconciliation is a set of practices for a specific group called Christians. Why Yom Kippur practices forgiveness in the way it does (and I am not sure

Pastor Lord has it right) relates to a people who live as Jews, not to Yom Kippur being a universal opinion about forgiveness which makes good psychological sense. See Michael Goldberg, *Jesus and Christians: Getting Our Stories Straight,* (Philadelphia: Trinity Press International, 1991).

8. Richard Rorty, *Contingency, Irony, and Solidarity* (Cambridge: Cambridge University Press, 1989). If rebellious ethics among Jews and Catholics was to be depicted in a novel, it could be done no better than in Erich Segal's *Acts of Faith* (New York: Bantam, 1992). Daniel's lapse from Judaism after writing his thesis on "Sexual Sublimation as a factor in Religious Faith," and Deborah's return to a touchy-feely Reform Congregation after her flight from the evils of stern Jewish Orthodoxy are religious romantic rebels personified. Unfortunately, the author is not trying to write comedy.

9. This point is made well by Alasdair MacIntyre in *A Short History of Ethics* (New York: MacMillan, 1966), 198. Can this be the vision of future clergy advocated by Henri J. M. Nouwen in his popular book on ministry, *The Wounded Healer* (Garden City, NY: Doubleday & Co., 1972)? "The Man who can articulate the movements of his inner life, who can give names to his varied experiences . . . This articulation, I believe, is the basis for spiritual leadership of the future, because only he who is able to articulate his own experience can offer himself to others as a source of clarification. The Christian leader is, therefore, first of all a man who is willing to put his own articulated faith at the disposal of those who ask his help" (32).

   Perhaps Nouwen's vision was some sort of reaction against pre-Vatican II Catholicism. Perhaps it was merely a mistake. At any rate, Pastor Lord appears to be the embodiment of "spiritual leadership for the future."

10. Martin Marty, "Clergy Ethics in America: The Ministers on Their Own," in *Clergy Ethics* (Louisville: Westminster/John Knox Press, 1991), 23–36.

11. Marty, 29. The history of the American Protestant clergy's move from public concern to individual care is beautifully documented by E. Brooks Holifield, *A History of Pastoral Care in America* (Nashville: Abingdon, 1983). For a concise critique of the way in which the contemporary discipline of Pastoral Care has, in general, debilitated clergy, see Karen Lebacqz and Archie Smith, Jr., "The Liberation of Language: Professional Ethics in Pastoral Counseling," *Quarterly Review,* Vol. V, No. 4, Winter 1985, 11–20.

12. George Lindbeck, *The Nature of Doctrine: Religion and Theology in a Post-Liberal Age* (Philadelphia: Westminster Press, 1984).

13. Peter Berger, *The Heretical Imperative* (Garden City, NY: Anchor Press, 1979).

14. I find it curious that even as astute a critic of social power arrangements as Letty M. Russell fails to see how her call for the contemporary church to overcome "paternalism" and to "demystify the structures" are forms of Sammons' "rebellious ethics" and thus an accommodation to the predominant configurations of social power rather than a defeat of them. Russell quotes with approval Richard Sennett's definition of authority as "a relational bond that leads persons to give assent without coercion or persuasion." What is a "relational bond" but an exchange of power between persons which is inherently coercive, although often subtly so? See Russell's "Authority in Mutual Ministry," *Quarterly Review,* Vol. 6, No. 1. Spring 1986, 10–23.

15. As James Gustafson has said, "Narratives function to sustain the particular moral identity of a religious (or secular) community by rehearsing its history and traditional meanings. . . . Narratives shape and sustain the ethics of the community . . . give shape to our moral character . . . deeply affect the way we interpret or construe the world . . . and thus affect what we determine to be appropriate action as members of the community." *Why Narrative?* eds. Stanley M. Hauerwas and L. Gregory Jones (Grand Rapids: Eerdmanns, 1989), 2–3.

16. *The Christian Century,* November 20–27, 1991, 1118.

17. MacIntyre has shown how important consistent, communally derived practices are for the cultivation of virtue. Through the practice of ritualized forgiveness in the Sunday liturgy, we become forgiving people. MacIntyre defines a practice as "any coherent and complex form of socially established cooperative human activity through which goods internal to that form of activity are realized . . . with the result that human powers to achieve excellence and human conceptions of the ends and goods involved are systematically extended" (*After Virtue,* 175).

18. In his *The Black Church in the African-American Experience* (Durham, NC: Duke, 1990), C. Eric Lincoln clearly sees that the privatized, individualized, psychologized style of clergy in predominately white churches is a function of politics and economics. Black clergy, according to Lincoln and his fellow author, Lawrence H. Mamiya, have never forsaken their corporate, communal style, sensing that their church existed in a hostile culture. Ministry as a personal matter is a sure sign of cultural accommodation. See

also Archie Smith, Jr., *The Relational Self: Ethics and Therapy From a Black Church Perspective* (Nashville: Abingdon, 1982).

19. Note that Jesus' "Be perfect" occurs immediately after his call to "Love your enemies and pray for those who persecute you" (Mt. 5:44).

20. Charles Taylor, *Sources of the Self: The making of Modern Identity* (Cambridge, MA: Harvard University Press, 1989).

21. Taylor, 217.

22. Taylor, 230.

23. It ought to make all the difference in clergy ethics that clergy witness to and act in light of a living God. As Hauerwas says,

> . . . the greatest immorality of the contemporary ministry is its willingness to substitute socialization for belief in God. Too often an implicit atheism is accepted or ministers do not believe their congregations can be held together by belief in God. Pastors fail to challenge the congregation to trust that God creates and sustains the church. As a result the church becomes the means of underwriting the dominant ethos of our culture . . . rather than being a people who think nothing is more important than worship of God. *Christian Existence Today,* 147.

24. See William H. Willimon, *Peculiar Speech: Preaching to the Baptized* (Grand Rapids: Eerdmanns, 1992).

25. Reverend Emmett's stress on the practical nature of forgiveness seems close to Stanley Hauerwas' account of forgiveness among the Mennonites in his "Reconciling the Practice of Reason," 67–87, *Christian Existence Today.*

26. James P. Wind, J. Russell Burck, Paul F. Camenisch, and Dennis P. McCann eds. (Louisville: Westminster/John Knox, 1991).

27. I have attempted to think about clergy ethics in this essay through narrative, juxtaposing the story of Pastor Lord with that of Reverend Emmett. I hope thereby to have demonstrated the value of narrative thinking as discussed by Stanley M. Hauerwas and David Burrell in "From System to Story: An Alternative Pattern for Rationality In Christian Ethics" in *Truthfulness and Tragedy: Further Investigations In Christian Ethics* by Stanley M. Hauerwas (Notre Dame, IN: University of Notre Dame Press, 1977), 15–39.

28. *The Book of Worship* (Nashville: The United Methodist Publishing House, 1992), 677. Kierkegaard, great philosopher of the personal, nevertheless saw clearly that ordination is the key to who pastors are, a powerful communal

act which has the grace to effect that which it celebrates: "A priest is essentially what he is through ordination, and ordination is a teacher's paradoxical transformation in time, by which he becomes, in time, something else than what is involved in the immanent development of genius, talents, gifts, and so forth." *Concluding Unscientific Postscript* trans. Walter Lowrie (Princeton: Princeton University Press, 1968), 244.

The Point of Serving

John C. Danforth

When I first came to the Senate in 1977, with the country still feeling the pain of the Watergate scandal, the Senate took up and passed an ethics resolution. Not long thereafter, the ethics resolution became the basis of the Ethics in Government Act. The resolution and the act are replete with rules that are meant to guide the ethical behavior of members of Congress, their staffs, and the Executive Branch, and there are now—nearly sixteen years later—thick books of advisory opinions and ethics offices staffed with legal counsel to offer guidance in the ways of the law. The rules explain when gifts may be accepted and when they may not, when meals and lodging may be paid for by someone else and when they may not, when transportation may be paid for and when it may not, and similar issues. These rules and opinions are meant to state the bounds of good behavior. They surely speak to concerns over political corruption and influence peddling. But they have very little to do with the ethical challenges faced by most politicians at the end of the twentieth century.

Recently, an unprecedented number of members of Congress decided not to run for reelection. Others were defeated in primary elections, and still others in the November elections. Those that remain are a troubled lot. Indeed, I have never heard more members of Congress express discontent with their jobs.

I have given some thought to the reasons for this, and I think there are several. The least significant reason is that nobody likes to be criticized and tarred with the brush of "Congressional perks." Nobody likes the pundits and the press to heap criticism all the time. No one likes that. This is human nature. The relentless criticism and various scandals and complaints get under the skin of politicians, and that may be a part of their discontent. But there is more to it than that.

I think the major cause is that deep down in our hearts most of us who serve in Congress believe that Congress has done something terrible and unforgivable to this wonderful country. Deep down in our hearts, we know that Congress has bankrupted America and given our children a legacy of bankruptcy.

We have been so intent on getting ourselves elected that year after year we have put off the hard issues. Year after year we have told people that they can have both more benefits *and* lower taxes.

We have done even more than that. We have gone to people and said: "You know, the great issue is fairness. You, the American people, are treated unfairly. You are asked to do too much. The burden is too heavy on you. If we listened to you, we would not treat you so unfairly. Do you know what is unfair? Your taxes are too high. Your benefits are too low. You are asked to shoulder too much of the burden."

That is the basic message we have given to the American people: "Feel sorry for yourselves because you are Americans. Your burden is too heavy." Is that not pitiful?

This is the first generation in the history of this country that has wanted to take more than it has given. And Congress continues to encourage this by saying, "Get us through the election. It is a Presidential year, and Senator So-and-So is up for reelection this year. Just get us through. No hard choices this year."

This was surely the message in 1992. It can be repeated in 1994 and 1996. We can go on, I am confident, for the rest of the terms of every person now serving in Congress because we have found some other person, some other group to hold the bag, even our own children. Let them worry about it.

The reason for discontent in Congress is not that politicians are being criticized. It is not that we have been tarred by somebody else's brush. It is not the fact that members of Congress now must pay a fee to use the Congressional gym, or whatever reforms are put in place. What trivial things those are.

I believe Senators and Representatives are discontented because in different ways and to varying degrees, each has been a part of decisions that have hurt this country, decisions that were driven by a desire to avoid difficult choices, to avoid political heat, and to make it easier to win reelection.

We who serve in Congress have told Americans that they should feel sorry for themselves, that they can have something for nothing, that we can reduce taxes and increase benefits even though the numbers do not add up.

Some people say the nation's problems would vanish if corrupt and incompetent people were not around. If only we did not pay members of Congress and Federal bureaucrats so much, so the story goes, the money would be available and we could have everything. If only we did not have foreign aid or lobbyists, if only we could keep cutting defense spending, we could spend the money. If only we did one thing or another, we would be able to spend more on ourselves and pay less in taxes.

This is fraud. It is a fraud perpetrated to make people happy and win their votes at the expense of their children and their children's children. It happens, I suspect, at every level of government, and it is very tempting to be part of this fraud because it holds out the promise of election. This temptation is a true ethical and moral challenge, and it has nothing to do with free parking spaces at National Airport, free plants from the Botanical Gardens, free tickets to ballgames, and the like. It has to do with telling the truth. Hard truths. Telling people things they do not want to hear but that we know to be true.

Conventional wisdom says government is out of touch and doesn't listen to people. I could not disagree more. Government is in *constant* touch. Politicians are forever taking polls, analyzing focus groups, worrying about the next election. Our ears are so close to the ground that we are unable to move. We are so fearful of making a mistake that we are unwilling to speak about, much less act on, the hard issues of our time.

The problem is not that we don't listen. The problem is *what we hear.* Our actions—or inactions—are governed by what we hear. In politics, as in other lines of work, the customer is always right.

More often than not, what politicians hear is the case for lower taxes and higher benefits; the unfairness of paying as we go; and the reasons to make difficult choices later, not now.

We also hear about the effects of interest group politics. But the interest group problem is widely misconceived. Interest groups are not trench-coat-wearing bagmen stuffing thousand dollar bills into the pockets of greedy politicians. Interest groups are *us.* Interest groups are the subsets of American society into which all of us have willingly placed ourselves.

"Interest groups" are veterans, farmers, workers, employers, small businesses, big businesses, senior citizens, gun owners, teachers, and members of more classifications of citizens than you can count. We all receive newsletters from Washington organizations that tell us they represent us, and we send them our money. We accept the description that we are members of a subculture, not a common American culture, that our group is being put upon, and that we must mobilize and stand up for our rights.

Some politicians are more than willing to exploit these differences in the name of getting elected. Politicians at all levels of government and of all political stripes are advised by pollsters and campaign consultants to seek out "wedge" issues, to stake out positions that will lay claim to one or more interest groups and, in the process, deny their support to the other candidate. This is "negative campaigning" in the truest sense of the word. As often as not, it entails the demonization of the opposition, the misrepresentation of the other side's views, and the grotesque simplification of complex and difficult social issues. It is rarely honest. In the pursuit of issues that divide us, it ignores our common interests and needs. But wedge campaigning has considerable political currency because, say the experts, it works. But at what price?

How can we act for the common good if we are so busy looking out for our own good? Is it any wonder that we can't balance the budget? Is it any wonder that the American people have come to distrust their own government?

The problem isn't that politicians don't listen. The problem is that they don't speak, or when they do, they don't tell us anything we, individually, don't want to hear. They treat us as what we have allowed ourselves to become—a series of interest groups, and little else.

Of course, the notion that America is comprised of competing economic and regional interests is not new. It was recognized by the framers of the Constitution and was the basis of the system of checks and balances that is the foundation of American democracy.

Nor is the acceptance of greed a novelty in American history. The quest for self-gain powers the engine of economic growth, and it is the essence of amazingly successful capitalist economies. The utopian dismissal of self-interest was the inherent flaw that led to the failure of Marxism.

And, surely, competition among groups serves democracy. Ambition for self drives economic growth. Any notion that we should or could free the country from group interest and personal ambition strikes me as just plain silly. The question is not whether humankind is divided and selfish. The question is whether there is anything else. Does anything transcend selfishness? Can each of us be called to rise above ourselves?

Self-interest is a powerful motive. But it is not the only motive for human action. Self-interest does not lead the Peace Corps volunteer to live in a hut in rural Senegal. Self-interest does not put the grate-patrol worker on the streets helping the homeless in the cold of winter. Self-interest does not prompt all kinds of people, black and white, young and old, to set themselves to the task of rebuilding Los Angeles with hammers and nails, brooms and mops. Self-interest has nothing to do with tutoring poor kids or visiting old folks or loving AIDS patients.

No one is a saint. But no one is wholly selfish, either. Ambition for personal self-gain does not suffice to make us whole persons. Pursuit of group interests does not suffice to make us a whole nation.

No group in America wants to pay higher taxes. No group in America wants to receive lower benefits. That is understandable. It is human nature. But the whole of America is greater than the sum of its interests. A $4 trillion national debt may be all right for a variety of specific interest groups. It is wholly wrong for America.

It saps the nation's strength. It steals the birthright of future generations. It transforms a proud land into one that begs for funds from
abroad.

If only there were simple answers. There are none. If only we could
find solutions in cutting waste or punishing corruption. We cannot. The
only ways to control the deficit are to raise taxes, cap entitlement programs, or, more likely, a combination of the two. Any suggestion that
there is a painless solution to the deficit problem is a fraud on the American people. Any suggestion that the social problems that plague America
can be resolved without sacrifice—or without each of us taking some
real measure of responsibility for ourselves, our families, and our communities—denies reality. We have to tell the truth.

The point is that it is not enough to live for oneself or for the here-
and-now. We have a duty to look beyond ourselves toward others, away
from the present toward the future and those who will come next. The
tendency to concentrate exclusively on the here-and-now is, I think,
the great fault of political debate in the late twentieth century.

Reinhold Niebuhr said, "Man's capacity for justice makes democracy
possible; but man's inclination to injustice makes democracy necessary."[1]
To Niebuhr, the Bible explains both the goodness of humankind, created
in the image of God, and the evil always present in our fallen state. We
are good enough to govern ourselves. That is what makes democracy
possible. We are sinful enough both to need government and to want to
twist government into our own purposes. That is what makes the re-
strained power of democracy necessary.

A familiar collect in the Episcopal *Book of Common Prayer* begins
with the phrase, "O Lord our Governor, whose glory is in all the
world: We commend this nation to *thy* merciful care" (p. 820). That, of
course, is the petition of each of us, that our future should be in God's
hands, and that His blessing be on our nation. Yet we who would serve
God in this country, in this world, have a duty not to stand and wait for
a blessing from above, but to move as God's active agents in God's dynamic world.

None of us has the wisdom to translate the will of God into policy positions on specific political issues, and each of us should be wary of those

who claim such divine inspiration. Religious duty is not discharged by taking stands on what we suppose are the right sides or what we think are the right issues. Religious duty includes living with humility, looking beyond our own interests and those of our own groups.

The ethical challenge that politicians face is to do just that: to live beyond the interests of our own survival, and to call the people we represent to live beyond themselves as well.

This may not be the path to electoral success. Quite likely, it is the opposite. But it is time to question the notion that candidates for political office can only get elected by setting people against each other, by exploiting division, by denying the truth, and by supporting proposals that make the country divided and weak. This requires hard choices. But I believe that those of us who are called to public service have a duty and an obligation to tell the truth, even if we lose. If we cannot get elected on such a basis, what is the point of serving?

NOTES

1. Reinhold Niebuhr, Children of Light and Children of Darkness (New York: Charles Scribner's Sons, 1944), xi.

Appendix:
Ethics Audit Worksheet

1. At the time your organization (i.e., your firm, company, etc.) was founded, what significant events or changes were taking place in your profession/industry? What significant events or changes have taken place in the profession/industry since then? What effects have they had on the way you do business and on your organization's ethics?

2. What have been the critical turning points in the history of your organization? How were things different following these turning points? What impact did such turning points have on your organization's "values"?

3. What themes or patterns can you discern in your organization's history, i.e., in its story? Which are associated with success and which with failure?

4. Which individuals have had the most impact on your organization's story? How? Have there been persons who, in terms of your organization's core values, might be viewed as exemplars or "saints"? How? Were there certain characteristics such people regularly displayed? If so, how did they enact such *virtues?*

5. What is the role of 'tradition' in your organization? Does the past shape the way your organization responds to present circumstances? How? Do people show regard or reverence for those who have come before them? If so, how?

6. What corporate institutional practices, ceremonies, or rituals most truly express your organization's values?

7. If there are organizational values that you would like to change, what practices, ceremonies, etc., would you start changing? What new practices, ceremonies, etc., would you introduce?

8. For each "stakeholder" in your organization—staff/employees/ colleagues, clients/customers, larger community—which specific "values" or ethics are you committed to practicing? What are the corresponding commitments you expect of each stakeholder?

9. Does your organization serve any purpose that transcends making money? If so, what is it? Is the world a better place because your organization is in it? How?

Contributors

John C. Danforth, Senior Senator (Republican) from Missouri, is a lawyer and an ordained Episcopal priest. His undergraduate degree is from Princeton University, and his degrees in theology and in law are both from Yale University. Prior to his election to the Senate in 1976, he served as Missouri's Attorney General.

Deborah Fernhoff, Ph.D. is a clinical psychologist and Director of the Atlanta Center for Psychotherapy, Inc. in Atlanta, GA. Her undergraduate degree is from Douglass College (Rutgers University), master's from Bryn Mawr College, and doctorate from Temple University. She is an avid reader of science fiction and hopes that if she cannot be the first psychologist in space she can at least write and be published in the science fiction field.

Michael Goldberg, an ordained rabbi with a doctorate in philosophy of religion and systematic theology, has served as Special Consultant to the Georgia Supreme Court and State Bar on professional ethics and has worked with the international strategic management consulting firm of McKinsey & Company. He is a founder and principal of Vision Design, a strategic planning consultancy to synagogues and churches.

Nancey Murphy, is Associate Professor of Christian Philosophy at Fuller Theological Seminary in Pasadena, CA, where she also teaches Christian ethics. She has doctorates in both theology and philosophy (specializing in philosophy of science), and is Chair of the Board of Directors of The Center for Theology and the Natural Sciences in Berkeley, CA.

Jack L. Sammons, Jr. is Professor of Law at Walter F. George School of Law, Mercer University. He is the author of *Lawyer Professionalism* and numerous articles on the ethics and the ethical regulation of the legal profession. Professor Sammons was a founding member of the Chief Justice's Commission on Professionalism. He lives in Macon, GA.

Theophus (Thee) Smith is Associate Professor of Religion at Emory University, Atlanta, GA. He is a graduate of St. John's College, Annapolis, Virginia Theological Seminary, and the Graduate Theological Union, Berkeley. He is the author of *Conjuring Culture: Biblical Formations of Black America* and co-editor of *Curing Violence: Religion and the Thought of Rene Girard.* Dr. Smith is also a consultant for groups engaged in welcoming diversity, prejudice reduction and conflict resolution, and is also active in multicultural-classical curriculum reform.

Richard P. Vance, M.D. is Associate Professor in the Department of Pathology and Coordinator of the Section on Medical Humanities, Office of Medical Education, at The Bowman Gray School of Medicine, Wake Forest, University, Winston-Salem, NC.

William H. Willimon is Dean of the Chapel and Professor of Christian Ministry at Duke University, Durham, NC. He is a graduate of Wofford College and earned his master's degree at Yale Divinity School and his doctorate at Emory University. He is the author of many articles and books, including *What's Right With the Church* and *Worship As Pastoral Care.* Dr. Willimon has given lectures and taught courses at many pastors' schools and at colleges and universities in the U.S., Canada, Europe, and Asia.